GIFTS TO MAKE FOR
SPECIAL OCCASIONS

GIFTS TO MAKE FOR SPECIAL OCCASIONS

Lyn Orton

HAMLYN

CONTENTS

This edition published in 1989 by the Hamlyn Publishing Group Ltd,
a division of the Octopus Publishing Group, Michelin House, 81
Fulham Road, London SW3 6RB.

© 1989 The Hamlyn Publishing Group Ltd
ISBN 0 600 56547 5
Produced by Mandarin Offset – printed in Hong Kong

Artists Bob Reed, Gilly Newman, Sally Ward
Photographer Sue Atkinson, Arc Studios
Stylist Janet Rhind-tutt
Production Controller Jenny May

To David, Tom and Sam for their love, and my sewing
machine for its performance. I would also like to
thank Ruth Goodman, Jenny Glew and Kathie Selwood
for their help and Pat Roberts for her enthusiasm and
encouragement.

The projects in this book combine simplicity of style and good design with a sense of humour – the emphasis has been on making presents that will be fun to give and to receive.

Some of the projects may only initially appeal to the experienced needlewoman. If you are not too confident about embarking on these more challenging projects, make up a dummy using inexpensive calico first. Then if you make any beginner's mistakes, you will not have wasted good fabric.

There are two points worth bearing in mind as you follow the instructions in this book. If you find the seam allowance given (1 cm/⅜ in) too narrow, and you would prefer to work on a wider turning, just alter the size of the cutting out patterns accordingly. On these cutting out patterns, notches are sometimes given as a reference for matching different pieces of material together – never cut into a pattern.

Anyone planning to make a lot of these gifts, would be well advised to take over the corner of a room, or even an entire room, if you can afford such a luxury. Here you will be able to keep all your sewing equipment together, leave the sewing machine and a half-sewn item out safely, and then return to them a few hours later without having to clear up everything whenever you stop. Make sure the work corner is large enough to accommodate your sewing machine, a cutting table and still leave you plenty of space to work comfortably. The light must be good and you should have easy access to an electric point.

Sewing machine

As the sewing machine will be your most useful and expensive piece of equipment, it pays to carefully investigate the market if you are buying a new one.

Buying a sewing machine

There are two important things to consider when choosing which sewing machine to buy: first, the variety of stitches you are likely to need, and second, how much time you will spend sewing by machine. You may need it only occasionally, but if you use it for several hours every week, you would be well-advised to look at machines in the middle to upper price bracket. Being good quality these will stand up to a lot of use. There are inexpensive machines which can perform more stitches than an expensive model, but the more costly version will have a longer life.

Where you buy your sewing machine is another important factor. A working demonstration from a helpful salesperson is invaluable, and good after-sales service is essential. Like any other mechanical device, sewing machines need servicing from time to time. It's also reassuring to know that if you have difficulty understanding part of the instruction book, you can go back and they will explain it to you. All too often I've heard someone say that they are not happy with the way their machine is working, only to find that it is the way it is being used that is at fault. Ask your friends where they purchased their sewing machines and if they have been satisfied with the service.

Your sewing machine specialist should be able to show you a range of machines to suit your requirements. Even so, try out several machines for yourself – take along scraps of different fabrics that you are likely to use. In this way you can see for yourself how each machine copes with a variety of materials. Trying the machines for yourself will also enable you to get the feel of the different models. Very few people would consider buying a car without test-driving it first to find out if they like the way it handles – the same applies to a sewing machine.

Choice of sewing machines

The most basic sewing machine is only capable of straight and zigzag stitching but comes in a range of prices offering varying quality. This may suit the occasional sewer who is only interested in making a few handicrafts.

The most popular machines have dressmaking stitches, that is buttonholer, blind hemming, stretch stitching and a choice of seam neatening to cope with a variety of fabrics. The most efficient form of seam neatening can be obtained from a separate overlocking machine. These are becoming increasingly popular with people who want a very professional finish perhaps because they intend to sell work at craft fairs. But as it involves buying a second machine, they are an extravagance, and not really worth the investment if you are only an amateur.

Dressmaking models fall into two basic categories – 2-dial and 3-dial machines. A 2-dial machine usually gives a choice of widths for zigzag stitches, but a set width for all the others. This may be a little easier to learn with, but does limit the machine's versatility, and you may get frustrated with it as you become more ambitious. A 3-dial machine has a changeable width on all stitches, with the exception of some models on which you will find that the length of buttonhole stitches is fixed.

There are very real advantages to machines that work electronically. They are capable of far greater needle penetration than conventional electric machines, which means that you can sew very thick and dense fabrics with ease. Some electronic models give greater control when you are slow stitching and are very easy to use.

Machines which have embroidery stitches usually offer a good range of dressmaking stitches as well, giving the user an opportunity to be a little more adventurous with her sewing.

Computer-driven machines are the simplest to use. Most have a considerable range of stitches, and the most complicated work can be done at the touch of a button. Even an inexperienced sewer will be able to do things that would have been difficult on other machines but they are the most expensive option.

Sewing machine problems

Some of the more common sewing machine problems can be easily rectified. When you start sewing, the machine may seem reluctant to get going and then shoot off faster than you expected, or the needle may become unthreaded. This is because the machine has been started off in the middle of a stitch, causing it partially to jam. Prevent this happening by ensuring that the cotton take-up lever is at its highest point before you place the fabric under the pressure foot. Hold both ends of the thread, while turning the balance wheel towards you until the cotton take-up lever has travelled to the bottom of its stroke and back to the top again. This ensures that your machine starts off correctly when you next press the foot control. On completing a seam, check that the cotton take-up lever is at its highest point before removing the fabric. The fabric will then release from the machine freely on two threads, not more. (The instruction manual will show you which is the cotton take-up lever and balance wheel.)

If your machine misses stitches, this is usually because the needle is blunt or unsuitable for the type of fabric. A range of different needles for every sewing machine are available, which vary not only in thickness but also in point-shape and coating. Ball point, stretch, perfect stitch and blue tip are all needles suitable for fabrics which have a large proportion of synthetic fibre in them, but only for a knitted fibre material, not a woven one.

Leather needles have a bladed point to enable them to cut cleanly through leather and suede. They can do serious damage to ordinary fabrics and should not be used on PVC if it has a fabric backing.

General equipment

Here is a guide to most of the basic sewing equipment you will need for making the projects in this book.

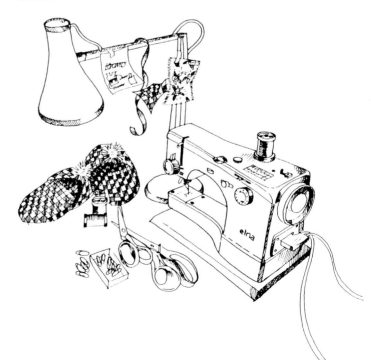

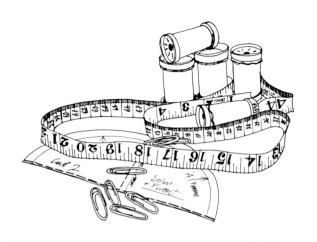

bedcovers and tablecloths. These will be approximately 19-25 cm (7¾-10 in) long, blade and handle included. The special design makes it easy to cut fabric accurately when it is laid on a flat surface.

You will need one pair of finely pointed sharp scissors (approximately 13-14 cm (5-5½ in) long), for notching, snipping cottons or tight corners, unpicking any mistakes and working at your sewing machine.

Take good care of your scissors. Never allow them to be used on card, paper or string or they will become blunt and try not to drop them on the floor too frequently. Keep an old pair of scissors for specially cutting out card and paper.

Cutting table

For cutting out fabrics, use a large hard-topped table that will not be spoiled by shears, and which is a good height for you to work at – the level of your elbow when you stand. Even a large piece of composition board fixed to a smaller ordinary table with adhesive plasticine will do.

If your sewing room has to double up as a bedroom, you could place a large piece of hardboard over the bed and use this as a cutting table.

Scissors

Always use good quality shears and scissors. Dressmakers' shears with raised handles and curved ends are essential when cutting large areas of fabric such as

Ruler, yardstick and tape measure

As well as a small transparent metric/Imperial ruler (essential for working on paper patterns), a transparent metric/Imperial yardstick would be useful when working on large areas of fabric. If a transparent yardstick is not available, a wooden or plastic one is an acceptable substitute.

You will also need a strong tape measure marked on one side in centimetres, on the other in inches. Ideally it should be made of glass fibre or a synthetic material so that it is not liable to stretch or tear and will be long-lasting.

When following the instructions for the projects in this book, only use one set of measurements for each gift – in other words, work in either metric or in Imperial, not in a mixture of the two.

8

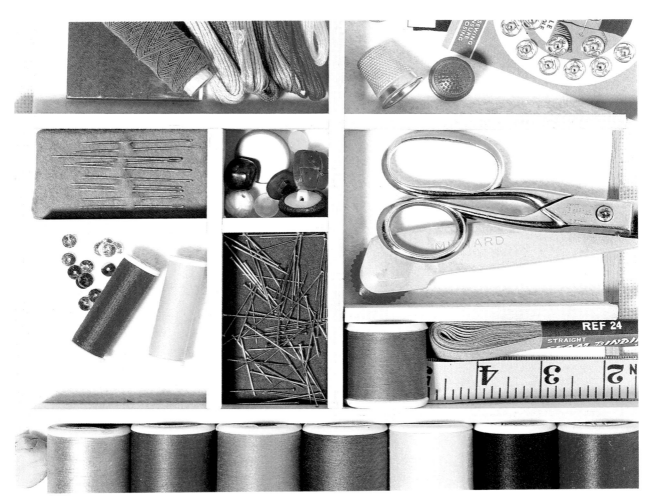

Threads

Experiment with good-quality threads to find which best suits your sewing machine. Always choose a slightly darker shade than the fabric. Keep a large reel of tacking cotton handy – using machine thread will prove expensive.

Tailor's chalk

White tailor's chalk is very useful when working on coloured fabrics, felts and so on, and 'bangs out' easily.

Beige tailor's chalk is more suitable for paler fabrics and will also bang out easily.

Needles

Fine needles must be used for fine fabrics.

Thick needles are suitable for coarser fabrics.

Betweens are short needles mostly used for intricate work.

Sharps are longer than betweens and used for most hand-sewing.

Thimble

A well-fitting metal thimble helps when working on canvas or any thick fabric. It protects your finger, and will speed up your sewing action too.

Pins

Use only the finest quality steel pins. Never use rusty pins as they will mark the fabric.

Glass 'bead-end' pins are very useful when joining very thick fabrics and are easy to locate.

White brass pins are particularly good for fine fabrics. They remain sharp for a long time.

General sewing box

It's always a good idea to have a general box for all your spools, tape measures, chalk, pins and other paraphernalia. Even a shoe box lightly padded with polyester wadding and covered with an oddment of curtain fabric will make attractive storage. Why not make several boxes and separately store items such as ribbons, tapes, bindings and velcro; artificial flowers; buttons; scissors, tracing wheel, fret saw and so on; threads and paper patterns.

Equipment for ironing

It is always a good idea to work with an iron and ironing board next to the sewing machine, so that pressing at each stage is not too inconvenient.

Iron

Ideally you should have a steam iron for pressing your handicraft work. Many of the fabrics used in this book – canvas and felt, for example – react best to steam. The iron should be small and lightweight so it fits easily into the tight corners on small craft items. A travelling model would be perfect. Always keep the sole of your iron spotlessly clean. There are several iron cleaners on the market which will melt away scorch and burn marks. Test your iron setting on a sample piece of the fabric on which you are working to make sure it is not too hot. Where possible, always press on the wrong side of the fabric to prevent shining or marking. Remove tacking stitches or pins before pressing or they will mark the fabric. Try to use the tip, rather than the iron's entire surface, and avoid over-pressing – you may damage the material.

Ironing board

A sturdy well-padded board is a pleasure to use. Cover your board with a small blanket and a large piece of cotton fabric. You will find a cotton cover is better than a polyester one as it will take the hottest setting.

Sleeve board

A sleeve board which is clipped on to the ironing board is essential to dressmaking but it is also helpful for when you are working on tiny areas. A small double-sided circle, for example, can easily slide over the smaller point of a sleeve board.

Pressing pads

These are invaluable when you are working on curved shapes and small craft items. Make your own by cutting two circles of fabric, the same size, using a round plate as a guide. Pin, tack and stitch the circles together, leaving a small opening, and then pad with polyester wadding to make a firm mound. Stitch the opening to close.

Pressing cloth

If you prefer working with a dry rather than a steam iron, keep a large square of washed cotton and a bowl of water to hand. Dampen the cloth and wring it out well before using it to press your work – it should not be too damp. Try not to have the iron too high or it will dry the pressing cloth as soon as it comes into contact with it.

Materials

The gifts in this book are all made from an imaginative and impressive array of materials, available from most good fabric or department stores. Below is a brief guide explaining which fabrics are suitable for which type of handicrafts.

The materials list at the beginning of each project does specify exactly what fabric was used to make the gift appearing in the photograph. But don't feel you have to keep strictly to our ideas. Part of the joy of handicraft design is coming up with your own colour schemes.

Interlinings

Bondaweb is a soft iron-on adhesive web with a special paper backing to make it easy to handle and cut. It is useful for bonding two fabrics together and is ideal for appliqué work and repairs.

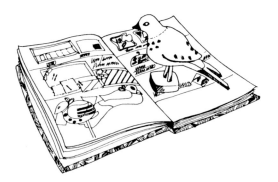

Polyester wadding is recommended throughout the book for light, even padding. Unlike some waddings, which disintegrate with use, this stays intact and washes well. It is available in three weights: light at 50g (2oz), medium at 100g (4oz) and heavy at 250g (8oz).

Vilene is used for backing. The best and thickest is craft-quality vilene, which has proved invaluable in the design of tablemats, bibs and cake frills. Iron-on vilene – adhesive on one side – is useful when you want a firm and neat finish.

Fabrics

Kiss-laminated PVC was originally designed for display work in shop windows, but the shiny surface and the splendid range of colours make it a wonderful fabric for using in handicraft work.

Cotton-backed PVC has a woven cotton backing and is suitable for clothing. It is used in clothes such as the painting dungarees and pinafore which need to be waterpoof and the Christmas apron, coasters and table mats and babies' bibs for easy cleaning. It is usually 1.5m (59in) wide.

Deckchair canvas/awning comes in a wide choice of colours and widths. It is extremely versatile and hard-wearing and can be used to make durable bags, swimming and travel packs and even a puppet theatre for hanging in a doorway.

Taffeta and bridal print are used throughout the wedding and christening chapter. They are much softer than white and compliment the complexion beautifully. Both the print and the plain taffeta are made from polyester – a silk taffeta would be expensive – but have the same exquisite rustle as silk taffeta which makes them a joy to wear.

Felt One of my passions is using felt, and the range of coloured felts available provides endless scope. It is an excellent fabric for handicrafts as it is easy to cut and doesn't fray. Unfortunately however as it is not particularly durable, it is only suitable for toys or decorative items – not clothing – like the advent snowman and the advent tree.

Fine fabrics such as voile are delicate, and best for things that will not be subjected to heavy use. The Christmas tree tablecloth is a good example. It is designed for

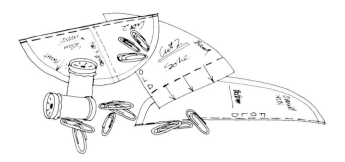

use just once or twice a year or a special occasion – an heirloom to treasure which can be carefully washed and put away for the next time.

Lamé is an exciting fabric for wedding anniversary gifts and evening wear. It is a 'fluid' fabric made from metallic fibres and so it needs a backing like iron-on vilene to fold it together.

Beads, ribbons, bells and sequins are invaluable for decorating craftwork. They are easily bought in most haberdashers, but it pays to build up your own collection, removing buttons from old clothes and saving left-over ribbon. Look out for bags of ribbon off-cuts, which are sold cheaply. Keep your collection in small glass jars with screw-top lids, so you can easily find what you need.

TODDLERS' BIRTHDAYS

Here are some exciting new ideas for toddlers on their birthdays: presents that are unusual enough not to be cast aside or to lie forgotten at the bottom of the toy box, only a few days after they have been unwrapped.

A circular bib made from blue, yellow and white striped PVC with a bold '1' motif would be quick and easy to make for a baby celebrating his or her first birthday. A year later stitch together a trough bib with a '2' motif, for the second birthday.

Another present you can make for meal times is the set of green and white striped PVC mats decorated with pink ice cream cones made from felt, polyester wadding and tiny coloured baubles. A matching mobile can be hung above the table to keep hungry people amused while the food is being prepared.

When a toddler is old enough to move from a cot to a bed, you can give him or her a cat and kitten bedcover. Made in easily washed glazed cotton chintz, this has a mother cat and three kittens attached to it with velcro. The position of the cat and kittens can easily be changed around, so this should keep early risers quiet for a while in the morning.

The most challenging projects in this chapter are the rainbow theatre and puppets – including a king, queen, peasant lady, page boy and soldier – on sticks. But once made these will provide endless hours of amusement at birthday parties.

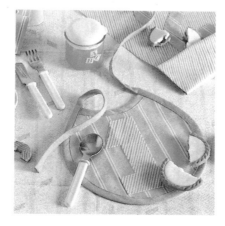

Right Three toddlers revel in the gifts which have been unwrapped at a birthday party. The rainbow theatre and some puppets are already hanging across a corner of the room and the ice cream mobile is suspended from the ceiling. PVC bibs hang from the door handle on the right, and then scattered in disarray on the floor are transport puppets, another PVC bib and one of the kittens from the cat and kitten bedcover.

Left A circular bib made from PVC, and decorated with a '1' motif.

RAINBOW THEATRE

This rainbow puppet theatre can provide the answer to rainy day blues or be the centre piece for children's parties. Let the kids come up with their own scripts or re-tell old favourites.

materials

25 cm (10 in) each of 129 cm (51 in)-wide kiss-laminated PVC in red, green, yellow and lime

3 m (3¼ yd) of 2.5 cm (1 in)-wide pale blue cotton bias binding

red gloss paint, undercoat, brush, sandpaper, wood adhesive

1.1 m (43 in) length of 1.5 cm (⅝ in)-diameter wooden dowel

2 turned wooden ends, or wooden doorknobs, 4.5 cm (1¾ in) diameter at base

8 cm (3 in) each of 90 cm (36 in)-wide awning canvas in red, yellow, orange, green and blue

60 cm (23½ in) each of 2.5 cm (1 in)-wide cotton bias binding in red, yellow, orange, green and blue

30 cm (11¾ in) of 115 cm (45 in)-wide deep blue polyester/cotton

2.2 m (86 in) length of 90 cm (36 in)-wide blue awning canvas

2 metal hooks

4 buttons, 3 cm (1¼ in) diameter

1 m (39½ in) lengths of 2 cm (¾ in)-wide satin ribbon in red, orange, yellow, green, and 2 blue lengths

1 oblong of cardboard 20 cm (8 in) × 40 cm (15¾ in)

1 m (39½ in) lengths of 5 mm (3/16 in)-wide ribbon in red, yellow, orange, lime green and blue

matching threads (red, orange, yellow, green, blue)

centimetre pattern paper

scissors, tailor's chalk, teflon foot, steam iron, pencil

to make

1 Transfer the diagrams for the frieze and the balloons to the centimetre pattern paper. Using these as your patterns, cut the following:
from laminated PVC 7 balloon shapes from assorted colours
from pale blue bias binding 4 × 44 cm (17¼ in) lengths, 2 × 23 cm (9 in) lengths, 1 × 60 cm (23½ in) length.

to dowelling using wood adhesive.

2 Sandpaper, undercoat and gloss paint the dowelling rod and ends. When dry, join the turned ends/knobs

3 Arrange the coloured canvas strips in order: red, orange, yellow, green, blue. With 1 cm (⅜ in) turnings, join the corresponding long edges to form the frieze oblong.

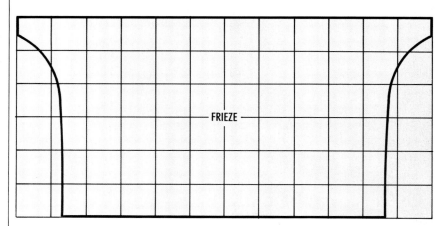

FRIEZE

Scale 1 square = 5 cm (approx 2 in)

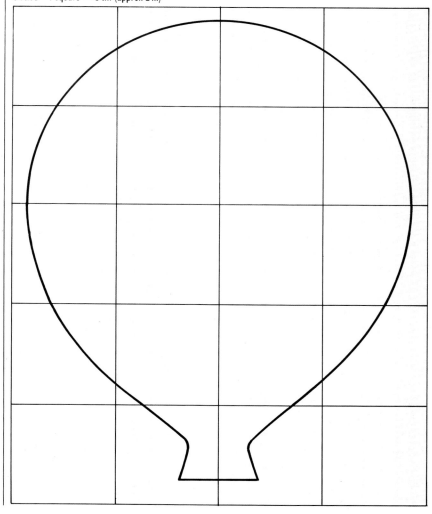

Blend the colours on the canvas frieze by covering the seams and top and bottom edges with the 60 cm (23½ in) lengths of matching bias binding. Match the folded raw edges of the bias binding to the seam lines on the front of the frieze and the red and pale blue binding to the top and base edges and topstitch.

4   With right sides together, place the blue polyester/cotton lining oblong over the completed canvas frieze. Pin, tack and trim away any excess lining fabric. Using the frieze pattern and turning at 'fold', use the tailor's chalk to mark the shape on the polyester/cotton side of the frieze. Tack along the chalk lines and machine stitch, beginning and ending at the notched opening. Trim away excess canvas and lining along each curved side, leaving 1 cm (⅜ in) turnings. Turn through to right sides. Roll out the seams and flatten the edges. Pin and tack to hold in place. Using a hot steam iron, press the edges down firmly.

5   On one short end of the long piece of blue canvas, turn an 8 cm (3 in) hem to wrong side. Pin, tack and machine stitch. Remove tacking.

6   Slide rod into top hem. Screw hooks into top of door frame and hang theatre length in an open doorway. Allowing canvas to just touch the floor, turn up a hem on lower edge. Pin. Remove theatre length and rod. Tack and top-stitch the hem. Remove tacking.

7   At a point approximately 47 cm (18½ in) down from the top hemmed edge, mark a 42 cm (16½ in) square centrally. Using sharply pointed scissors, snip into one of the top corners. Cut across top and down sides. Do not destroy the edge of the square or cut the base line. This flap will be the 'stage' of the puppet theatre.

8   Turn up a 1 cm (⅜ in) hem at each end of two of the 44 cm (17¼ in) lengths of binding and wrap the folded sides evenly over the vertical raw edges of the stage opening. Pin, tack and machine stitch on the extreme edge of the folded binding, stitching through all thicknesses. Repeat for the top horizontal edge using a 44 cm (17¼ in) length. Remove tacking.

9   Bind top horizontal raw edge of 'stage' flap with one 44 cm (17¼ in) length of blue bias binding. Form the 'drawbridge stage' by folding the 42 cm (16½ in) flap in half, with the bound top edge touching the underside of the

folded front. Pin and tack side edges together. Wrap each of the two 23 cm (9 in) lengths of bias binding over the double thickness raw side edges of the stage in the same way as the opening. Do not machine stitch the folded edge of flap.

10   Sew 2 buttons to the underside of stage flap, approximately 3 cm (1⅛ in) from folded edge as in the step-by-step illustrations on this page. Sew the other 2 buttons to the back of the canvas theatre. Position them approximately 30 cm (11¾ in) from the top folded edge and 22 cm (8½ in) in from the left and right selvedges. (These will support the ribbon lengths and hold the 'draw-bridge stage' flat.)

11   With blue polyester/cotton side of frieze to front of canvas theatre, match base of frieze to bound top edge of stage opening. Pin, tack and topstitch. If your machine cannot take the thickness of the canvas, either handsew or join with parallel lines of velcro.

12   Place the wrong side of the laminated balloon shapes as photograph, leaving the 'neck' of each balloon free. Pin, tack and topstitch using the teflon foot and working on the extreme edge of balloon shapes. Remove tacking.

Tie lengths of contrasting narrow ribbon round necks of balloons.

13   Slide cardboard oblong into the open bound long edge of the stage flap.

14   Slide the finished rod into the top hem of the canvas theatre. Hang rod on the hooks. Loop the two blue ribbons over the buttons at the corners of the stage. When the stage is level, loop the other end of ribbons over buttons at back of theatre, knot to secure. Arrange the remaining 2 cm (⅞ in) wide lengths of red, orange, yellow, green ribbons on pole.

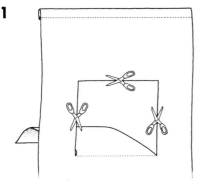

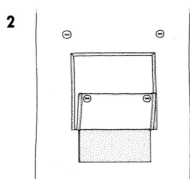

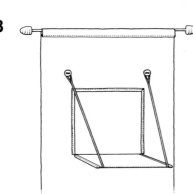

1   With tailor's chalk, mark a 42cm (16½in) square, 47cm (18in) from top edge of theatre. Cut down the two sides and along top.

2   Form stage floor, by folding cut-out flap in half. Pin and tack its sides together. Conceal raw edges with bias binding. Slide cardboard into open long edge of stage floor.

3   Loop one end of each blue ribbon over buttons under rear corner of stage. With stage level, secure other ends of ribbons to buttons along top edge of stage opening.

PUPPETS ON STICKS

A royal family and their court make colourful puppets on felt-covered sticks for the rainbow theatre. Add to their entourage by adapting the instructions to make princes and princesses, a whole army of soldiers or a fairy godmother to act out stories which are familiar to the children.

Curtains up!

KING

materials

27 cm (10½ in) × 18 cm (7 in) craft-quality vilene
22 cm (8½ in) square red felt
27 cm (10½ in) × 18 cm (7 in) red kiss-laminated PVC
14 cm (5½ in) square polyester wadding
23 cm (9 in) × 14 cm (5½ in) gold lamé bondaweb
fabric and water-based adhesive
31 cm (12 in) length of 1 cm (⅜ in) square wooden rod
28 cm (11 in) × 4.5 cm (1¾ in) yellow felt
8 cm (3 in) polystyrene ball
30 cm (11¾ in) square lightweight polyester wadding
31 cm (12 in) square muslin or pale pink stocking fabric
4 silver beads, 1 gold bell
matching thread (red, white)
2 blue beads, 1 red bead
1 m (1 yd) of 1.2 cm (½ in) wide green satin ribbon
centimetre pattern paper
ballpoint pen, scissors, craft knife

to make

1 Join all identical lamé pieces (2 crowns) with bondaweb.
2 Transfer the diagrams for the king to centimetre pattern paper. Using these as your patterns, cut out the following pieces:
vilene underskirt, red felt robe, red kiss-laminated PVC cloak, polyester wadding beard, gold lamé crown doubled on bondaweb.
3 Apply a good coat of water-based adhesive to 28 cm (11 in) of the 31 cm (12 in) wooden rod and fabric adhesive to 28 cm (11 in) length of yellow felt.

When tacky, place rod on adhesive side of felt and roll up slowly, smoothing as you work, and cover rod. Leave one end of rod free of felt for 3 cm (1 in).
4 Using a craft knife or the points of sharp scissors, carve a 1 cm (⅜ in) square out of the polystyrene ball shape.
5 Push some adhesive into the square hole, slide in wooden (uncovered) end of rod and leave to set.
6 Secure the centre of 30 cm (11¾ in) square of polyester wadding to the top of the ball head of puppet with a pin. Pull the polyester wadding down to neck and secure by binding with thread. Leave excess polyester wadding to form shoulders. Tie knot to hold. Using muslin or pale pink stocking fabric, repeat the process.

to dress

Position red felt robe on vilene. Pin, tack and machine stitch 6 mm (¼ in) seam round neck and down centre back. Sew on silver beads to front of robe as in photograph. Wrap robe round king, pin and tack down centre back. Catchstitch to close. Remove tacking. Wrap red kiss-laminated PVC cloak and secure at centre front, exposing silver beads. Pin and tack beard in position. Position crown over sides of beard. Overlapping centre backs of crown, pin, tack and catchstitch to hold. Sew on blue beads for eyes and a red one for nose.

to finish

Trim away any excess vilene which might show along the hems of the puppet. Thread gold bell on 1 m (1 yd) length of satin ribbon and criss-cross stick handle of puppet as shown below.

Scale   1 square = 5 cm (approx 2 in)

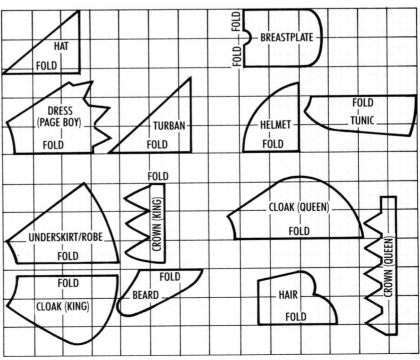

QUEEN

materials

22 cm (8½ in) square craft-quality vilene
22 cm (8½ in) square white felt
22 cm (8½ in) square gold lamé
22 cm (8½ in) square silver lamé
bondaweb
2 × 30 cm (11¾ in) squares lightweight
   polyester wadding
23 cm (9 in) × 10 cm (4 in) silver lamé
fabric and water-based adhesive
31 cm (12 in) length of 1 cm (⅜ in) square
   wooden rod
28 cm (11 in) × 4.5 cm (1¾ in) red felt
8 cm (3 in) polystyrene ball
31 cm (12 in) square muslin or pale pink
   stocking fabric
5 gold stars, 1.5 cm (⅝ in) diameter
3 gold beads
matching thread (silver, gold, white)
2 blue beads, 1 pink bead, 1 gold bell
elasticated gold thread
pink felt tip pen
1 m (1 yd) of 1.2 cm (½ in)-wide white satin
   ribbon
centimetre pattern paper
ballpoint pen, scissors, craft knife

to make

1 Join identical lamé pieces (crown, cloak) with bondaweb.
2 Transfer the diagrams to centimetre pattern paper. Using these as your patterns, cut out the following:
vilene underskirt, white felt robe, gold and silver lamé cloak doubled on bondaweb, polyester wadding hairpiece, silver lamé crown doubled on bondaweb.
   Follow Steps 3-6 on page 17.

to dress

Decorate an area down centre front of white felt robe piece with gold stars and gold beads. Make robe as king's robe and attach. Wrap gold lamé cloak lined with silver round queen. Catchstitch at centre front, exposing stars and beads. Position polyester wadding hairpiece, joining centre line as diagram. Pin and tack. Wrap doubled lamé crown round head. Pin and catchstitch to hold. Sew on 2 blue beads for eyes and a pink one for nose. Tie gold thread round neck in bow. Colour cheeks with felt tip pen. Finish as for king.

PAGE BOY

materials

17 cm (6½ in) × 27 cm (10½ in) craft-quality
   vilene
22 cm (8½ in) square pink felt
2 × 22 cm (8½ in) squares turquoise
   felt
10 cm (4 in) square polyester wadding
fabric and water-based adhesive
31 cm (12 in) length of 1 cm (⅜ in) square
   wooden rod
28 cm (11 in) × 4.5 cm (1¾ in) lime green
   felt
8 cm (3 in) polystyrene ball
30 cm (11¾ in) square lightweight polyester
   wadding
31 cm (12 in) square muslin or pale pink
   stocking fabric
1 large 2 cm (¾ in) bead for hat
2 blue beads, 1 pink bead
matching thread (pink, turquoise)
pink felt tip pen
gold bell
1 m (1 yd) of 1.2 cm (½ in)-wide mauve satin
   ribbon
centimetre pattern paper
ballpoint pen, scissors, craft knife

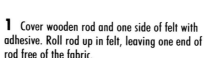

1 Cover wooden rod and one side of felt with adhesive. Roll rod up in felt, leaving one end of rod free of the fabric.

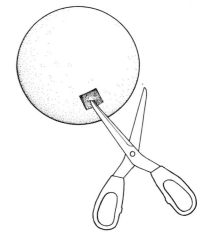

2 Using a pair of scissors or a craft knife, carve a small square hole out of the polystyrene ball which forms the puppet's head.

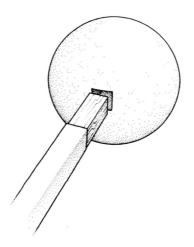

3 After putting fabric adhesive in square hole of head, slide the uncovered end of the wooden rod into it. Leave to dry.

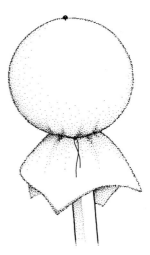

4 Secure polyester wadding to puppet head with pin. Pull down and secure around puppet's neck by binding with thread. Knot.

to make

1 Transfer the diagrams to centimetre pattern paper. Using these as your patterns, cut out the following: vilene underskirt, pink felt robe, hat and 4 small triangles for robe decoration, polyester wadding hairpiece.
Follow Steps 3-6 on page 17.

to dress

Make robe as for king and attach. Arrange felt triangles on hem and secure with fabric adhesive as in picture. Wrap turquoise felt square to form cloak, dropping top corner to form the collar. Catchstitch centre front to hold. Join hat from point to curved edges. Pin and tack. Catchstitch or machine stitch carefully. Remove tacking.

Sew polyester wadding hairpiece to head, joining at marked seam. Place hat on hair. Pin, tack and catchstitch to hold. Sew large bead to point. Sew on blue beads for eyes and pink bead for nose. Colour cheeks with felt tip pen. Finish as for king.

PEASANT LADY

materials

28 cm (11 in) × 17 cm (6½ in) craft-quality vilene
22 cm (8½ in) square turquoise felt
2 × 22 cm (8½ in) squares blue felt
22 cm (8½ in) square lime green felt
fabric and water-based adhesive
31 cm (12 in) length of 1 cm (⅜ in) square wooden rod
31 cm (12 in) × 4.5 cm (1¾ in) pink felt
8 cm (3 in) polystyrene ball
30 cm (11¾ in) square lightweight polyester wadding
31 cm (12 in) square muslin or pale pink stocking fabric
7 small acrylic balls, 1 cm (⅜ in) diameter
2 green beads, 1 pink bead, 1 gold bell
pink felt tip pen
1 m (1 yd) of 1.2 cm (½ in)-wide yellow satin ribbon
matching thread (blue, turquoise)
centimetre pattern paper
ballpoint pen, scissors, craft knife

to make

1 Transfer the diagrams to centimetre pattern paper. Using these as your patterns, cut out the following: vilene underskirt, turquoise felt robe, lime green felt turban triangle.
Follow Steps 3-6 on page 17.

to dress

Repeat robe and cloak (a complete blue felt square) as page boy. Arrange turban triangle of felt on head, overlapping in front as photograph. Pin, tack and catchstitch. Using fabric adhesive, glue on small acrylic balls to form collar. Sew on beads for eyes and nose. Colour cheeks with pink felt tip pen. Finish as for king.

SOLDIER

materials

28 cm (11 in) × 34 cm (13¼ in) craft-quality vilene
50 cm (20 in) × 2 cm (¾ in) craft-quality vilene
2 × 22 cm (8½ in) squares leaf green felt
2 × 26 cm (10¼ in) × 20 cm (8 in) silver lamé
2 × 20 cm (8 in) × 10 cm (4 in) silver lamé bondaweb
48 cm (19 in) × 2 cm (¾ in) yellow felt
fabric and water-based adhesive
31 cm (12 in) length of 1 cm (⅜ in) square wooden rod
28 cm (11 in) × 4.5 cm (1¾ in) turquoise felt
8 cm (3 in) polystyrene ball
30 cm (11¾ in) square lightweight polyester wadding
31 cm (12 in) square muslin or pale pink

stocking fabric
15 cm (6 in) × 2 cm (¾ in) polyester wadding
2 blue beads, 1 red bead, 1 gold bell
27 cm (10½ in) × 3.5 cm (1⅜ in) silver lamé
27 cm (10½ in) length of 6 mm (¼ in)-diameter wooden dowel
1 m (1 yd) of 1.2 cm (½ in)-wide yellow satin ribbon
matching thread (green, yellow)
centimetre pattern paper
ballpoint pen, scissors, craft knife

to make

1 Join identical lamé pieces (soldier's helmet and tunic) with bondaweb.
2 Transfer the diagrams to centimetre pattern paper. Using these as your patterns, cut out the following: vilene tunics, 2 green felt tunics, lamé breastplate and lamé helmet both doubled on bondaweb.
Follow Steps 3-6 on page 17.

to dress

Place vilene tunic pieces together. Pin, tack and machine stitch shoulder seams. Remove tacking. Repeat with green felt tunic. Slide felt and vilene tunics over soldier's head. Fuse the 48 cm (19 in) × 2 cm (¾ in) strip of yellow felt to bondaweb. Do not remove paper backing. Cut two 16 cm (6¼ in) lengths. Point ends, remove paper backing and place straps in X-shape on front of lamé tunic.

Slide double lamé breastplate over head, catchstitch to green tunic.

Cut the remaining 16 cm (6¼ in) length of fused yellow felt. Halve lengthways to form two 1 cm (⅜ in) bands. Peel off paper backing and arrange as photograph on front of helmet. Topstitch. Fringe top ends by snipping.

Wrap helmet round head, overlapping centre backs slightly. Pin, tack and catchstitch. Remove tacking. Sew on beads for eyes and nose. Knot the 15 cm (6 in) × 2 cm (¾ in) length of polyester wadding to form moustache, and catchstitch under nose.

Spear Apply adhesive to silver lamé strip and 6 mm (¼ in) dowel. When tacky, roll and smooth lamé on to dowel to cover. Catchstitch spear to silver tunic. Finish as for king.

TRANSPORT PUPPETS

Children will have hours of fun with these colourful transport puppets. They can make them sail, fly, chug or roar, and will love providing all the appropriate sound effects. The puppets are easy to make so you could use them as going home gifts after a party. No sewing is needed – just a lot of sticking. Felt cut-outs are glued to vilene backing and held aloft on felt-covered dowelling.

AEROPLANE

materials

22 cm (8½ in) square emerald green felt
22 cm (8½ in) square buttercup yellow felt
22 cm (8½ in) square sky blue felt
scraps of scarlet felt
15 cm (6 in) of 82 cm (32¼ in)-wide craft-quality vilene
22 cm (8½ in) length of 6 mm (¼ in)-diameter wooden dowel
fabric adhesive
centimetre pattern paper
scissors, ruler, ballpoint pen

to make

1 Transfer the diagrams to centimetre pattern paper. Using these as your patterns, cut the following:
from emerald green felt 2 main body aeroplane pieces
from buttercup yellow felt 2 main wings, 2 shortened wings, 2 tail wings
from sky blue felt 2 right and 2 left body strips, 4 propellers, 1 strip measuring 22 cm × 3.5 cm (8½ × 1⅜ in) for stick
from scarlet felt scraps 2 nose covers
from vilene 1 complete aeroplane shape, 16 oval window shapes.
2 Glue the pieces to the basic vilene shape in the following order, using fabric adhesive: (1) green main body (2) blue body strips (3) 8 vilene windows (4) yellow main wing, shortened wing and tail wing (5) 2 blue propellers (6) red nose cover. Refer to the photograph for positioning of pieces. You will need half the pieces for one side, the remainder for the other side. Repeat for the other side.
3 Cover the dowelling and the blue

felt strip with fabric adhesive. With a firm rolling action, wrap the dowelling with felt, overlapping the edges slightly. Catchstitch top 5 cm (2 in) of covered dowelling to one side of puppet.

BOAT

materials

22 cm (8½ in) square buttercup yellow felt
22 cm (8½ in) square sky blue felt
22 cm (8½ in) square emerald green felt

Scale 1 square = 5 cm (approx 2 in)

22 cm (8½ in) square scarlet felt
20 cm (8 in) of 82 cm (32¼ in)-wide craft-quality vilene
22 cm (8½ in) length of 6 mm (¼ in)-diameter wooden dowel
fabric adhesive
centimetre pattern paper
scissors, ruler, ballpoint pen

to make

1 Transfer the diagrams for the boat to the centimetre pattern paper. Using these as your patterns, cut the following shapes:
from buttercup yellow felt 14 curved hull strips
from sky blue felt 2 masts, 2 birds, 2 sets of outer waves
from emerald green felt 2 sets of inner

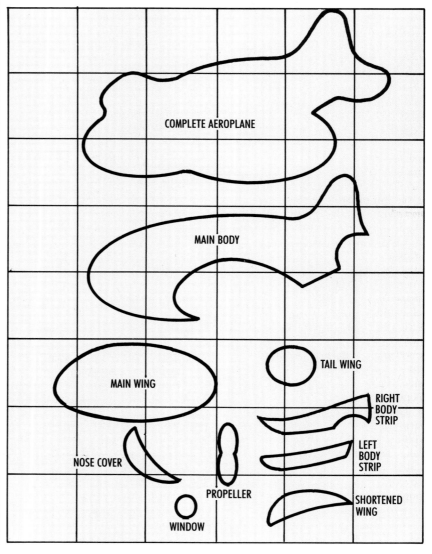

COMPLETE AEROPLANE

MAIN BODY

MAIN WING

TAIL WING

RIGHT BODY STRIP

LEFT BODY STRIP

NOSE COVER

PROPELLER

SHORTENED WING

WINDOW

waves
from scarlet felt 4 portholes, 2 pennants, 1 strip measuring 22 cm × 3.5 cm (8½ × 1⅜ in) for the stick
from vilene 1 complete boat with waves shape.

2 Using fabric adhesive, glue 7 yellow strips to the side of the boat, beginning at the base and overlapping to the deck. Then glue the pieces to the basic vilene shape in the following order: (1) a set of green inner waves (2) blue mast, bird and outer waves (3) 2 red portholes and 1 pennant. Refer to the photograph for positioning the pieces. You will need half the pieces for one side, the remainder for the other side. Repeat for the other side.

3 Cover the dowelling and the red felt strip with fabric adhesive. With a firm rolling action, wrap the dowelling with felt, overlapping the edges slightly. Catchstitch the top 5 cm (2 in) of covered dowelling to one side of the puppet.

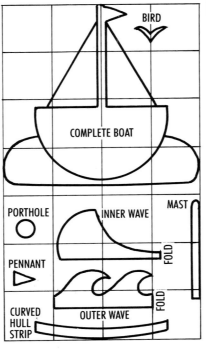

BIRD

COMPLETE BOAT

PORTHOLE   INNER WAVE   MAST

FOLD

PENNANT

FOLD

CURVED HULL STRIP   OUTER WAVE

Scale 1 square = 5 cm (approx 2 in)

CAR

materials

22 cm (8½ in) square sky blue felt
22 cm (8½ in) square buttercup yellow felt
22 cm (8½ in) square scarlet felt
15 cm (6 in) of 82 cm (32¼ in)-wide craft-quality vilene
22 cm (8½ in) length of 6 mm (⅜ in)-diameter wooden dowel
fabric adhesive
centimetre pattern paper
scissors, ruler, ballpoint pen

to make

1 Transfer the diagrams to the centimetre pattern paper. Using these as your patterns, cut the following:
from sky blue felt 2 car shapes
from buttercup yellow felt 2 front mudguards, 2 back mudguards, 2 front headlights, 1 strip measuring 22 cm × 3.5 cm (8½ × 1⅜ in) for stick

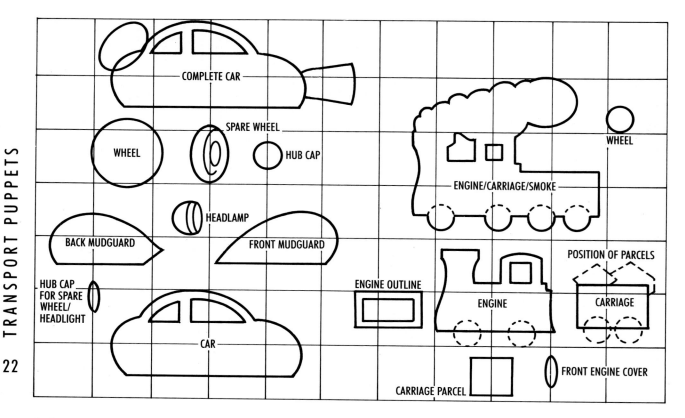

Scale 1 square = 5 cm (approx 2 in)

from scarlet felt 4 round hubcaps, 2 oval hubcaps (spare wheel), 2 headlamps
from vilene 1 complete car, 2 spare wheels, 4 wheels

2 Using fabric adhesive, glue the pieces to the basic vilene shape in the following order: (1) blue car (2) vilene wheels (3) red hubcaps (round) (4) yellow back mudguard (round) (5) yellow front mudguard (long) (6) vilene spare wheel (7) red spare tyre hubcap (8) red headlamp (9) yellow front headlight. Refer to the photograph for positioning the pieces. You will need half the pieces for one side, the remainder for the other side. Repeat for the other side.

3 Cover the dowelling and the yellow felt strip with fabric adhesive. With a firm rolling action, wrap the dowelling with felt, overlapping the edges slightly. Catchstitch the top 5 cm (2 in) of covered dowelling to one side of the puppet.

TRAIN

materials

22 cm (8½ in) square scarlet felt
22 cm (8½ in) square buttercup yellow felt
22 cm (8½ in) square sky blue felt
22 cm (8½ in) square emerald green felt
15 cm (6 in) of 82 cm (32¼ in)-wide craft-quality vilene
22 cm (8½ in) length of 6 mm (⅜ in)-diameter wooden dowel
fabric adhesive
centimetre pattern paper
scissors, ruler, ballpoint pen

to make

1 Transfer the diagrams to the centimetre pattern paper. Using these as your patterns, cut the following:
from scarlet felt 2 engines
from buttercup yellow felt 2 carriages, 2 outlines of engines, 2 front engine covers
from sky blue felt 8 wheels, 1 carriage parcel
from emerald green felt 1 strip measuring 22 cm (8½ in) × 3.5 cm (1⅜ in) for the stick, 1 carriage parcel

from vilene 1 engine/carriage/smoke shape.

2 Using fabric adhesive, glue the pieces to the basic vilene shape in the following order: (1) red engine (2) yellow engine outline (3) yellow engine front cover (4) blue parcel (5) green parcel (6) yellow carriage (7) 4 blue wheels. Repeat for the other side, omitting the two parcels. Refer to the photograph for positioning the pieces. You will need half the pieces for one side, the remainder for the other side.

Repeat for the other side.

3 Cover the dowelling and the green felt strip with fabric adhesive. With a firm rolling action, wrap the dowelling with felt, overlapping the edges slightly. Catchstitch the top 5 cm (2 in) of covered dowelling to one side of the puppet.

CAT AND KITTEN BEDCOVER

Mother cat sits proudly in the centre of the bedcover while her kittens play around her. They're attached with velcro so children can have lots of fun moving them about. The mother cat is lightly padded with polyester wadding, the kittens are 'bagged out', with topstitched eyes, noses and whiskers.

materials

MOTHER CAT

50 cm (20 in) length 1.5 m (59 in)-wide grey striped glazed cotton chintz
50 cm (20 in) length 1 m (39½ in)-wide light-weight polyester wadding
30 cm (11¾ in) length 2 cm (¾ in)-wide grey velcro
matching thread (grey, terracotta, lime green)
centimetre pattern paper
tailor's chalk, pencil, scissors

KITTENS

25 cm (10 in) length 1.5 m (59 in)-wide grey striped glazed cotton chintz
25 cm (10 in) length 1.5 m (59 in)-wide terracotta glazed cotton chintz
25 cm (10 in) length 1.5 m (59 in)-wide white glazed cotton chintz
6 × 6.5 cm (2½ in) lengths 2 cm (¾ in)-wide velcro, two each in pale grey, tan, white
matching thread (pale grey, terracotta, lime green, white)
centimetre pattern paper
tailor's chalk, pencil, scissors

to make

MOTHER CAT

1 Transfer the diagrams to the centimetre pattern paper. Using these as your patterns, cut the following:
from striped chintz 2 body circles, 2 face circles, 4 cheeks, 4 ears, 4 paws, 2 tails
from polyester wadding 1 body circle, 1 face circle, 2 cheeks, 2 ears, 2 paws, 1 tail.
2 Tear apart the 30 cm (11¾ in) velcro strip and position the hook half on the right side of one chintz body circle (see diagram). Pin, tack and machine stitch in place. Remove tacking.
3 With right sides together, place matching pairs of all the fabric shapes (body, face, cheeks, ears, paws and tail) with a corresponding polyester wad-

ding shape. Place wadding to one wrong side. Pin, tack and machine stitch through the three layers with 6 mm (¼ in) turnings, leaving the shapes open between the notches. Snip seams

Scale 1 square = 5 cm (approx 2 in)

around curves and angles. Remove tacking. Turn each piece through to the right side, rolling the seams out. Pin and tack round all pieces to hold flat, turning in seam openings. Catchstitch opening together for all pieces except body pieces.
4 Turning the edges on the notched opening on the body inwards, slide the straight edges of each paw into the

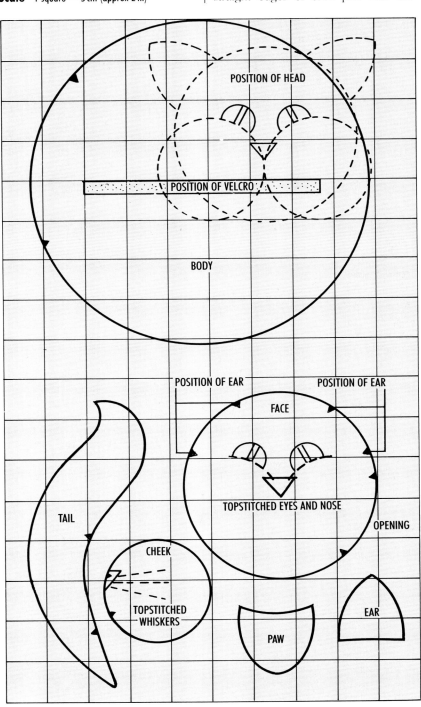

body circles. Pin, tack and topstitch 6mm (¼in) round the edge of the whole body circle. Remove tacking.

5 Position tail as in photograph. Pin, tack and topstitch inside edge. Remove tacking.

6 Pin and tack ears in position on head circle. Position head as in diagram. Pin, tack and topstitch around entire outside edge of circle, leaving ears free.

7 Position cheek circles on head. Pin and tack. Topstitch around half of each circle, starting under the point of nose position and ending where cheek circles meet top edge of head circle.

8 Fold cheek circles back and pin out of the way. Using lime green thread, outline the two eye half-circles. With a small zig-zag stitch, work across eye shapes, filling in the half circles. Mark the vertical lines in the cat's eyes with a close satin stitch worked in grey thread. Using terracotta thread, outline the nose shape. With a small zig-zag stitch fill in the nose outline. Using terracotta and a large zig-zag stitch, mark the whiskers from nose across cheeks.

KITTENS

1 Transfer the diagrams to centimetre pattern paper. Using these as your patterns, cut out the following.

from each chintz colourway 2 body circles, 2 face circles, 2 half-circles for eyes, 4 cheeks, 4 ears, 4 paws, 2 tails.

2 Each kitten has two 6.5cm (2½in) lengths of matching velcro on the back body circle. Tear apart the two 6.5cm (2½in) lengths of velcro for each kitten and position both hook halves on the right side of one body circle. Pin, tack and machine stitch.

3 With the right sides of all the matching fabric pairs together, pin, tack and machine stitch with 6mm (¼in) turnings, leaving an opening between the notches. Snip into the curves or angles. Remove tacking. Turn each piece of kitten through to the right side, rolling out seams. Pin and tack each shape flat.

4 Turn in the seams at the notched opening and catchstitch the openings together, with the exception of the body circles, which should remain open to take the paws.

5 Turning the edges on the notched opening on the body inwards, slide the straight edges of each paw into the body circles. Pin, tack and topstitch 6mm (¼in) round the edge of the

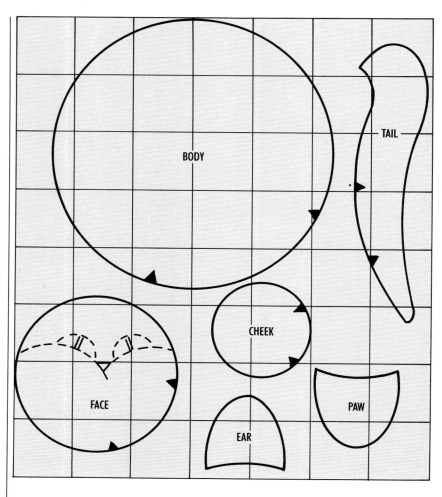

Scale 1 square = 5 cm (approx 2 in)

whole body circle. Remove tacking.

6 Pin and tack the ears to the back of the double face circle as in photograph.

7 Attach the face to the body. Position the face, again following photograph.

8 Pin, tack and topstitch the cheeks to each kitten's face circle at the extreme edge (see diagram). Parts of the cheek will overlap the edge, but continue the

ZIG-ZAG SATIN STITCH

To fill the crescent-shaped 'eyes' on the cat bedcover, mark the outline with a line of straight stitching. Using a closed zig-zag stitch, form vertical bars. Allow the fabric to move freely. Try out your stitches on a sample piece of fabric first before starting work on the bedcover.

line of topstitching.

Using a contrasting or matching thread (grey, terracotta, white) outline and then fill in the triangular nose shape, using a small zig-zag. Stitch single lines of zig-zag for the whiskers.

Using lime green thread and working from the diagram, machine stitch two half-circles above the cheeks on each face for the eyes. Fill each half-circle using a small zig-zag stitch. Mark vertical lines in the kitten's eyes with a close satin stitch worked in grey thread.

9 Pin and tack the tail to the left side of the front body. Topstitch 6mm (¼in) from the edge. Remove tacking.

10 Decide on the position of the cat and the kittens on the bedcover and attach the corresponding loop halves on the velcro to the cover. If you wish, put on extra velcro loops so the children will be able to attach the cat and kittens to the other parts of the cover.

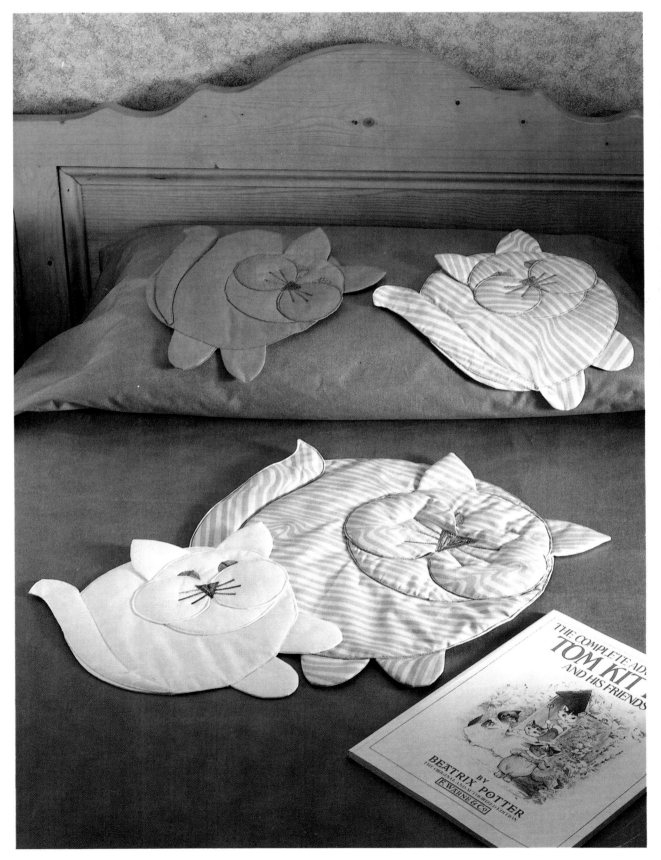

TROUGH BIB

These ample PVC bibs with their deep troughs will catch all the crumbs and dribbles – even from two-year-olds. They are easy to wipe clean and the strong bias binding ties soften the neck edge. Make two bibs, perhaps varying the pattern given here for blue bib with yellow '2' motif to make a yellow bib with a blue number.

materials for 1 bib

25 cm (10 in) × 145 cm (57 in)-wide blue-and-white striped cotton-backed PVC

16 cm (6¼ in) × 12 cm (4¾ in) printed toning PVC

12 cm (4¾ in) length of 2 cm (¾ in)-wide sky-blue velcro

75 cm (29½ in) of 2.5 cm (1 in)-wide deep yellow bias binding

centimetre pattern paper

matching thread (yellow, blue)

pencil, sellotape, scissors, ruler, teflon foot

to make

1 Transfer the '2' motif and the oblong bib pattern to centimetre pattern paper. Using these as your pattern, cut out the bib shape from the striped blue-and-white PVC and one motif shape '2' reversed on to the cotton side from the printed toning PVC. Cut two 6 cm (2⅜ in) lengths of velcro.

2 Take the bib shape you have just cut out and measuring down from the neck end, mark two points at 28.5 cm (11¼ in) and 21 cm (8¼ in). Place a hook and loop strip of velcro vertically down from these points on each side of the bib. There should be a 1 cm (⅜ in) gap between each hook and loop piece. Pin, tack and machine stitch the strips to the PVC. Remove tacking. (When the velcro is pressed together, it forms the trough.)

3 To attach the motif to the front, place the base of the motif approximately 31 cm (12 in) from the lower short edge of the bib. Sellotape the '2' motif centrally to the PVC. Using the teflon foot, machine stitch all round the motif 2 mm (¹⁄₁₆ in) from the edge. Remove the sellotape before it makes the PVC sticky.

4 Turn a 15 cm (6 in) hem to the back

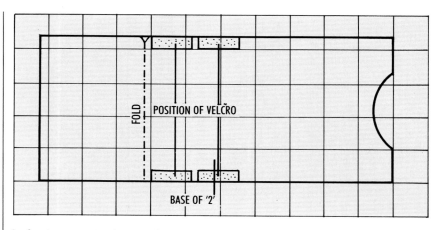

POSITION OF VELCRO

FOLD

BASE OF '2'

Scale 1 square = 5 cm (approx 2 in)

of the bib. Secure with a machine-stitched line across the width and down the sides of the hem approximately 3 mm (⅛ in) from the edge.

5 To neaten the neckline and make the bib's neck ties, fold the bias binding in half and match its centre point to the centre front of the bib. Fold the binding evenly over the neck shape and working through all thicknesses, tack the binding in place. Machine stitch from one end to the other, turning in 1 cm (⅜ in) at each end to neaten. Remove tacking.

6 Press the velcro together to form a trough.

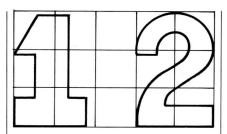

Scale 1 square = 5 cm (approx 2 in)

This special gift for a one-year-old is made from a simple circle of cotton-backed PVC big enough to protect the baby's birthday outfit. The '1' motif is cut from co-ordinated PVC and machine-topstitched in position. Soft bias binding covers the entire edge and makes neck ties long enough to hold the bib securely in place.

materials

25 cm (10 in) square yellow-and-white striped cotton-backed PVC

16 cm (6¼ in) × 12 cm (4¾ in) striped toning PVC

130 cm (51¼ in) of 2.5 cm (1 in)-wide blue bias binding

matching thread (yellow, blue)

centimetre pattern paper

pencil, sellotape, scissors, ruler, teflon foot

to make

1 Transfer the bib on page 82 and '1' motif to centimetre pattern paper. Using these as your patterns, cut out the bib shape from yellow-and-white PVC and the '1' motif from toning PVC. Cut one 115 cm (45 in) and one 15 cm (6 in) length of bias binding.

2 To attach the motif to the bib, place the base of the '1' approximately 3 cm (1¼ in) from the lower edge. Sellotape it to the PVC and, using the teflon foot, machine stitch all round, 2 mm (¹⁄₁₆ in) from the edge. Remove the sellotape.

3 Bind the neckline. Fold the 15 cm (6 in) length of bias binding in half and match the centre point to the centre front of the bib, folding the binding evenly over the neck shape. Working through all thicknesses, tack and machine stitch the binding to the neckline. Remove tacking.

4 Fold the 115 cm (45 in) length of bias binding in half and match the centre point to the bottom centre front of the bib. Fold the binding evenly around the entire edge of the bib, leaving 25 cm (10 in) free at each neck edge to form ties. Pin the binding in place, tack and machine stitch, turning a 1 cm (⅜ in) hem at each end of the binding to neaten. Remove tacking. The bib is complete.

ICE CREAM MOBILE AND MATS

Children's tea time will be more fun with these pretty place mats decorated with frothy ice cream cones, and a matching mobile to hang over a festive party table. The sugar-pink cones are frothing over with 'whipped' wadding, decorated with acrylic pom-pons and suspended from striped ribbon.

MOBILE

materials for 13 cones

3 × 22 cm (8½ in) squares sugar pink felt
60 cm (23½ in) square turquoise blue felt
75 cm (29½ in) of 1 m (39½ in)-wide light-weight polyester wadding
31 cm (12 in) of 1 m (39½ in)-wide heavyweight polyester wadding
12 m (12½ yds) of 3 mm (⅛ in)-wide striped ribbon
matching thread (blue, pink)
13 small acrylic pom-pons 1 cm (⅜ in) in diameter (pink, blue, green and yellow)
half of a circular wooden embroidery hoop 13 cm (5 in) in diameter
acrylic baubles, 2 cm (¾ in) in diameter (pink and yellow)
centimetre pattern paper
scissors, ballpoint pen, ruler

to make

1 Transfer the diagram to the centimetre pattern paper. Using this as your pattern, cut 13 triangles from pink felt. Cut six 4 cm (1½ in)-wide strips from the square of blue felt. (There will be some blue felt left over.)

Cut 13 triangle shapes from lightweight wadding and cut the remainder of this wadding into strips 4 cm (1½ in) wide by 1 m (39½ in) long. Cut 13 strips from the heavyweight wadding, each 6 cm (2⅜ in) × 20 cm (8 in). Divide the ribbon as follows: two 60 cm (23½ in) lengths for hanging the mobile; one 2 m (80 in) length to cover the ring and 13 varied lengths, one for each cone.

2 To quilt the felt, pin the lightweight wadding cones to the felt cones. Tack and topstitch, beginning at the pointed end and working in horizontal lines

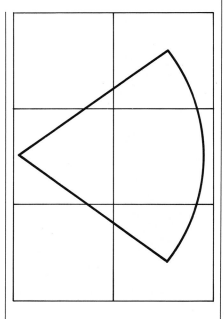

Scale 1 square = 5 cm (approx 2 in)

across each shape, leaving 6 mm (¼ in) between each line. Continue to the top of the cone. Remove tacking. Repeat for each cone.

3 To form the cone, roll up each cone so that the quilted felt is inside. Pin, tack and machine stitch down the long raw edges using a 6 mm (¼ in) seam. Remove tacking. Repeat for each cone.

4 Turn each cone through to the right side. Using the strips of heavyweight wadding, pad each cone shape, allowing the wadding to froth over the top of the cone. Catchstitch wadding 'ice cream' to the top of each felt cone. Catchstitch a coloured pom-pon to the top of the froth on each cone.

5 Using the various lengths of ribbon, catchstitch one end of each length to the top of each cone.

6 Cover the embroidery hoop with the remaining lengths of lightweight wadding. Pin and catchstitch the beginning of each strip as you work.

7 Cover the wadding on the ring with the strips of blue felt, catchstitching as you bind. Wrap the 2 m (80 in) length of ribbon round the ring to cover the edges of the felt strips.

8 Place each length of ribbon holding an ice cream cone on the ring, arranging them evenly around the circle so that the weight is balanced. Tie the

lengths of ribbon to the ring and make small bows for decoration. Catchstitch the ribbon to the ring to hold it securely.

9 Take the two 60 cm (23½ in) lengths of ribbon and tie each end evenly to opposite sides of the ring. Catchstitch for extra strength.

MATS

materials for 3 mats

35 cm (13¾ in) of 150 cm (59 in)-wide cotton-backed green-and-white striped PVC
35 cm (13¾ in) of 150 cm (59 in)-wide cotton-backed green PVC
35 cm (13¾ in) of 82 cm (32¼ in)-wide craft-quality vilene
22 cm (8½ in) square of sugar pink felt
22 cm (8½ in) square of lightweight polyester wadding
scraps of heavyweight polyester wadding
matching thread (pale green, pink)
4 × 1 cm (⅜ in)-diameter acrylic pom-pons
centimetre pattern paper
ruler, pencil, ballpoint pen, scissors, sellotape, teflon foot

to make

1 Transfer the diagrams to the centimetre pattern paper. Using this as your pattern, cut the following:
from striped PVC 1 mat oblong: 45 cm (17¾ in) × 33 cm (13 in), 1 × 18 cm (7 in) diameter circle
from green PVC 1 mat oblong: 47 cm (18½ in) × 35 cm (13¾ in), 2 × 20 cm (8 in) diameter circles, 2 × 24 cm (9½ in) diameter circles
from vilene 1 mat oblong: 45 cm (17¾ in) × 33 cm (13 in).
from pink felt 4 cone triangles
from lightweight wadding 4 cone triangles

2 To make the oblong mat, match the vilene oblong to the cotton side of the striped PVC oblong. Pin and tack as close to the edge as possible.

Cut away a 1 cm (⅜ in) square from each corner of the green PVC oblong. Cover the vilene side of the smaller oblong with the cotton side of the green oblong. Using sellotape, wrap the corners over on to the striped side of the mat oblong and neaten each corner.

Sellotape all the edges to hold flat.

Using the teflon foot, topstitch across both widths and lengths of mat oblong. Remove sellotape.

3 To make the circular mats, match the two 24 cm (9½ in) green circles with cotton backs together. Pin, tack and topstitch a double line round edge of mat. Remove tacking.

4 With cotton backs together, match the two smaller green PVC circles. Pin and tack. With the cotton side of the smaller striped mat to one PVC side of the tacked mat, position centrally. Pin,

tack and topstitch 6 mm (¼ in) from edge of striped circle. Remove tacking.

5 To make ice cream cones, position each wadding cone shape on each felt cone shape. Pin, tack and topstitch beginning at pointed base and working across the cone shape, with 6 mm (¼ in) spaces between each line. Continue topstitching to top of cone. Remove tacking.

6 With quilted felt side of cone to the inside and the long edges together, close seams with 6 mm (¼ in) turnings.

Pin, tack and machine stitch. Remove tacking. Repeat for all four cones. Turn cones through to right side.

7 Using the scraps of heavyweight wadding, pad each cone shape and allow wadding to froth over the top of the cone as in photograph. Catchstitch 'ice cream' made of leftover lightweight wadding to top of felt cone. Catchstitch pom-pon to top of ice cream cone.

8 Catchstitch two cones to oblong mat, one cone to large round mat and one to small round mat.

CHILDREN'S BIRTHDAYS

Jelly and cake alone will not keep kids happy at a birthday party. They need entertainment as well. Make some animal masks for them to clown around in. There is a lamb with his four-leaf clover, the cat and his fishbone, a rabbit eating a carrot and a koala. All these faces are made in coloured felt and will fit comfortably around any head with the help of a flexible velcro fastening. Decorate the tea table with messenger birds, perhaps putting one in each place setting and writing the child's name in the tag. Or use one of the birds as a novel birthday card, scribbling your message in the tag.

As far as a present for the birthday child is concerned, give someone who has just started at nursery school a pair of PVC painting dungarees or a pinafore. Make a cloth from a spare square of gingham and attach it to the pinafore or dungarees for wiping messy hands.

If the birthday is during the colder months, you could knit one of the woolly hats, and then have fun adorning it with fluffy yellow chicks, a large multi-coloured pom-pon or knitted holly for Christmas time.

In summer a swimming pack might go down well. There are two slightly different designs: one for a girl and one for a boy, though they are, of course interchangable. The dog pyjama case – a pure white dog sporting a smart red collar, sitting on a black and white spotted background – will be greeted with great enthusiasm by any child.

30

Right Among the jellies, potato crisps, chocolate biscuits and fizzy drinks on the tea table you can just get a glimpse of some birthday presents. An animal mask resembling a hare hangs on the back of the chair and messenger birds decorate the table. The birthday boy is already trying on his PVC painting dungarees – perhaps in anticipation of a wild party!
Left Three small girls playing in the garden with their animal masks: a cat, a lamb and a hare.

PVC PAINTING CLOTHES

A bright blue pinafore (chest size 58cm/23in) and shiny red dungarees (64cm/25in) provide protection for the budding artist or the child who can't resist splashing in puddles. The detachable straps are secured with velcro and the bagged out construction means that they really are paint proof! The patterns can be made larger or smaller by increasing or decreasing as necessary.

PINAFORE

materials

50cm (20in) of 150cm (59in)-wide blue cotton-backed PVC
1 m (39½in) of 115cm (45in)-wide red-and-white gingham
20cm (8in) of 1.5cm (⅝in)-wide sky blue velcro
matching thread (blue, white)
4 red buttons, 2cm (¾in) diameter
centimetre pattern paper
scissors, ruler, ballpoint pen, teflon foot

to make

1   Transfer the diagrams to centimetre pattern paper. Using these as your patterns, cut the following:
from blue PVC 1 front on the fold, 1 back on the fold, 2 straps
from gingham 1 front on the fold, 1 back on the fold, 2 straps, 1 × 37cm (14½in) square
from velcro 5 strips, each 4cm (1½in) long.
2   Take four of the velcro strips and position the loop pieces on the right side of the gingham straps (see diagram). Pin, tack and machine stitch. Remove tacking. Position each corresponding hook piece of velcro to the right side of the PVC pinafore front and back bodice (see diagram). Pin, tack and machine stitch. Remove tacking.
3   Position the fifth loop length of velcro diagonally across the right side of one corner of the raw-edged gingham square, approximately 5cm (2in) from the raw edges.
4   Place the right side of one gingham strap to the right side of one PVC strap,

beginning and ending at the notched openings. Pin, tack and machine stitch with 6mm (¼in) turnings. Turn through the opening to the right side. Roll out the edges of the strap and use tacking stitches to hold them flat. Topstitch strap 6mm (¼in) from edge. Repeat for the other strap.
5   Carefully sew the buttons to the PVC straps, covering the stitched area over the velcro. Avoid taking too much thread to the velcro side. (It is not possible to sew the buttons on before machining the straps.)
6   Match the front and back pinafore pieces with right sides together and with 1cm (⅜in) turnings. Pin, tack and machine stitch. Remove tacking and turn through to the right side.
7   Make up the gingham lining as for

Scale   1 square = 5cm (approx 2in)

PVC part of pinafore. Keep to wrong side.
8   Place the right side of the gingham lining to the right side of the pinafore. With 1cm (⅜in) turnings, pin, tack and machine stitch round the arm shapes and across the front and back. Remove tacking. Trim the turnings to 6mm (¼in) and snip into the curves of the arm shapings. Turn the gingham lining over to the inside of the PVC pinafore. Flatten the seam, then pin, tack and topstitch 6mm (¼in) from the pinafore edge. Remove tacking.
9   Turn a 1cm (⅜in) hem to the wrong side of the PVC pinafore. Pin, tack and topstitch 6mm (¼in) from the edge. Turn a 1cm (⅜in) hem twice on the gingham lining. Pin, tack, and machine stitch. Remove tacking.
10   Turn a 6mm (¼in) hem, then a 1cm (⅜in) hem on each side of the gingham square. Pin, tack and machine stitch. Remove tacking. Position straps and attach square to the velcro.

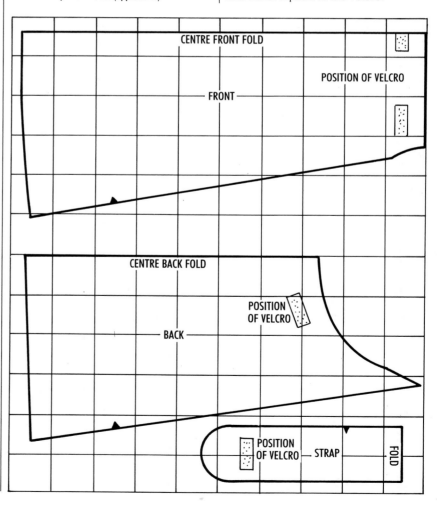

DUNGAREES

materials

1 m (39½ in) of 150 cm (59 in)-wide red
cotton-backed PVC
1.2 m (47 in) of 115 cm (45 in)-wide red-and-
white gingham
25 cm (10 in) of 1.5 cm (⅝ in)-wide white velcro
centimetre pattern paper
scissors, ruler, ballpoint pen, teflon foot

to make

1 Transfer the diagrams to centimetre
pattern paper. Using these as your
patterns, cut the following:
from red PVC 2 fronts, 2 backs, 2 straps
from gingham 2 fronts, 2 backs, 2 straps,
1 × 37 cm (14½ in) square
from velcro 5 strips each 5 cm (2 in) long.
Follow Steps 2-4 for the pinafore on
page 32.
5 Place the two PVC front pieces right
sides together. Pin, tack and machine
stitch down the centre front seam.
Repeat for the back pieces. Remove all
the tacking.
6 Join the front and back pieces at the
inner leg seam. With the right sides
together, match the raw edges and with
1 cm (⅜ in) turnings, pin, tack and
machine stitch in one continuous line
up one inner leg seam and down the
other. Remove tacking.
7 Taking 1 cm (⅜ in) turnings, pin, tack
and machine stitch both side seams.
Remove tacking.
8 Make up the gingham lining as for
the PVC part of the dungarees (Steps
5–7), but leave the inner leg seam open.
Make sure you keep the lining to the
wrong side.
9 Place the right side of the PVC
dungarees to the right side of the
gingham lining. With 1 cm (⅜ in) turnings, pin, tack and machine stitch round
the arm shapes and across the front and
back. Trim the turnings to 6 mm (¼ in)
and snip into the curves of the arm
shaping.
10 Slide the gingham lining up and
over the bib edge to the wrong side of
the PVC dungarees, turning them carefully and 'pointing out' the corners.
Push both lining legs down one PVC
leg. Pleat the PVC leg up and pull out
the gingham legs. Flatten the gingham

leg shapes carefully and match the raw
edges with 1 cm (⅜ in) turnings. Pin,
tack and machine stitch the inner leg
seam of the gingham lining in one
continuous movement. Remove tacking
and press seams flat. Pull out one
gingham leg and slide it into the
corresponding PVC leg.
11 Folding the dungaree legs up to
expose the cotton side of the PVC, turn
2 cm (¾ in) hems to the wrong side. Pin
and tack. Turn a 1 cm (⅜ in) hem twice
on the gingham dungarees. Pin and
tack. Slide the gingham lining over on
to the wrong side of the PVC: 1 cm
(⅜ in) of PVC will protrude. Pin, tack

Scale 1 square = 5 cm (approx 2 in)

and machine stitch on the folded edge
of the gingham hems. Turn the finished
legs to approximately 5 cm (2 in) deep.
Remove tacking.
12 Turn the lined straps on the marked
fold to reveal the pointed gingham
ends. Sew each button to the marked
position, sewing through all thicknesses
for strength. Match the hook and loop
pieces of velcro.
13 Turn a 6 mm (¼ in), then a 1 cm
(⅜ in) hem on each side of the gingham
square. Pin, tack and machine stitch.
Remove tacking.
14 Attach the straps and gingham
square for wiping messy hands to the
dungarees with the velcro. The dungarees are now ready to wear.

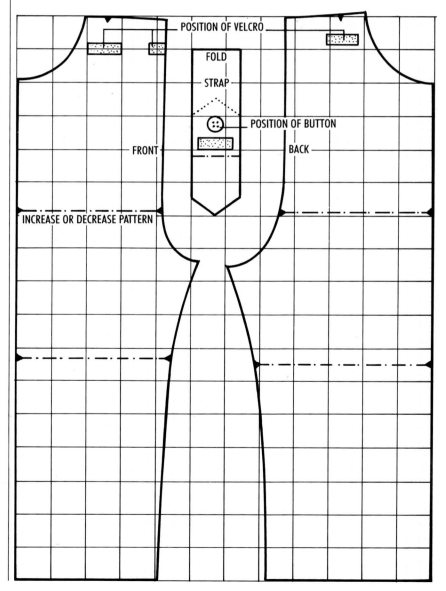

ANIMAL MASKS

These cheeky animal faces – a cat, lamb, hare and koala – are all made from felt and craft-quality vilene, following the same basic method. Let the kids invent a party entertainment, wearing them either indoors or out in the garden in the summer.

CAT

materials

60 cm (23½ in) square pale orange felt
22 cm (8½ in) square saffron yellow felt
22 cm (8½ in) square silver grey felt
22 cm (8½ in) square coral pink felt
30 cm (11¾ in) of 82 cm (32¼ in)-wide craft-quality vilene
20 cm (8 in) square lightweight polyester wadding
8 cm (3 in) of 2 cm (¾ in)-wide saffron velcro
matching thread (orange, pink, grey)
1 sequin
centimetre pattern paper
scissors, pencil, tailor's chalk, ruler

to make

1 Transfer the diagrams to centimetre pattern paper. Using these as your pattern, cut the following:
from pale orange felt 2 mask shapes, 2 cheek circles
from yellow felt 2 headband strips, 6 crooked strips
from grey felt 1 fishbone
from pink felt 2 inner ear shapes, 2 nose shapes
from vilene 1 mask shape
from wadding 2 cheek circles, 1 nose shape.
2 Pin and tack the hook and loop pieces of velcro to one end of each headband strip, horizontal to long edges and 1 cm (⅜ in) from short end. Machine stitch. Remove tacking.
3 Pin, tack and machine stitch the centre forehead dart in both pale orange felt mask shapes and the vilene interlining. Slit and lightly press felt darts open. Trim vilene dart down to 3 mm (⅛ in) turnings. Remove tacking.
4 Matching dart turnings on front felt mask to dart seam on vilene mask, pin

and tack through both dart seams. Smooth out felt mask, matching outer edges. Position one end of each felt headband piece to sides of mask as diagram, making sure that hook and loop lengths face each other to join at back of head. Pin and tack around mask edge, catching in headbands.
5 Pin and tack the corresponding polyester wadding cheek circles to the two pale orange cheek circles.
6 Position three of the crooked strips across the forehead of the cat as in the diagram. Pin, tack and topstitch close to edges. Cut the three remaining crooked

Scale 1 square = 5 cm (approx 2 in)

strips in half and arrange three on each cheek (see diagram). Pin, tack and topstitch close to edges. Remove tacking.
7 With wadding side of cheeks to cat's face, pin, tack and topstitch close to edges. Remove tacking.
8 Position the pink inner ears as diagram. Pin, tack and topstitch close to edges. Remove tacking.
9 Position fishbone across cat's face. Pin, tack and catchstitch in place. Remove tacking. Sew sequin eye to fish head.
10 Pin and tack polyester wadding nose between the two pink felt noses. Tuck in any visible wadding and topstitch close to edge. Catchstitch nose to cat's face as diagram.
11 With wrong sides facing, match the second felt mask shape to the vilene

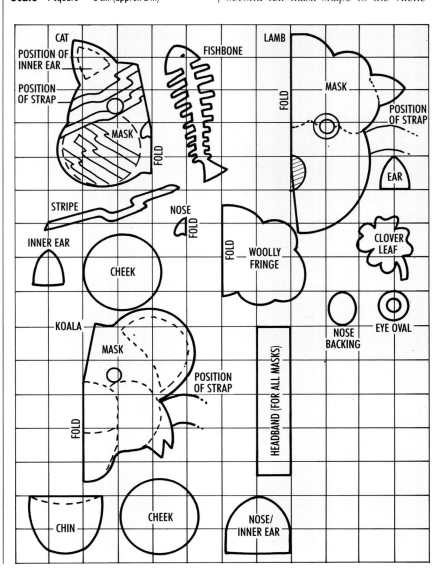

mask. Pin and tack in position, matching all edges. Topstitch 3 mm (1/8 in) round mask shape. Remove tacking.

12 Using orange thread, satin-stitch around eye. Carefully trim away the felt lining and vilene eye. Cut open the bottom half of the remaining top felt eye to make the eyelid.

LAMB

materials

60 cm (23½ in) square white felt
22 cm (8½ in) square black felt
22 cm (8½ in) square silver grey felt
22 cm (8½ in) square moss green felt
25 cm (10 in) of 1 m (39½ in)-wide lightweight polyester wadding
15 cm (6 in) of 1 m (39½ in)-wide medium weight polyester wadding
35 cm (13¾ in) square of craft-quality vilene
1 black plastic oval nose
8 cm (3 in) of 2 cm (¾ in)-wide white velcro
matching thread (white, black, grey, moss green)
centimetre pattern paper
scissors, pencil, tailor's chalk, ruler, fabric adhesive

to make

1 Transfer the diagrams for the lamb to centimetre pattern paper. Using these as your patterns, cut the following shapes:
from white felt 2 mask shapes, 2 headband strips
from black felt 1 nose backing, 2 ears
from grey felt 2 eye ovals
from moss green felt 2 clover leaf shapes
from lightweight wadding 1 mask shape
from medium weight wadding 1 'woolly fringe'
from vilene 1 mask shape.

2 Pin and tack hook and loop pieces of velcro to one end of each headband strip, horizontal to long edges and 1 cm (⅜ in) from short end. Machine stitch. Remove tacking.

3 Pin, tack and machine stitch the centre chin dart in both white felt mask shapes and the vilene interlining. Slit and lightly press felt darts open. Trim vilene dart down to 3 mm (1/8 in) turnings. Remove tacking.

4 Pin and tack the vilene mask shape to

the lightweight wadding mask shape (there is no need for a dart in the wadding). Pin and tack one felt mask to the wadding, wrong side facing the wadding and matching outer edges. Position one end of each felt headband piece to the sides of mask, making sure the velcro lengths face each other to join together at the back of the head. Pin and tack in place.

5 Position grey eye ovals over eye holes. Pin, tack and topstitch.

6 Match black ears to white felt ears. Pin, tack and topstitch close to edge.

7 Pin, tack and topstitch the clover leaves together, 3 mm (1/8 in) from edges. Remove tacking. Trim top leaf down to machine line. Position on lamb's face as in the photograph. Pin and catchstitch clover leaf to lamb's face.

8 Pin and catchstitch the black nose backing in position. Glue plastic nose in position.

9 With wrong sides facing, match the second white felt mask shape to the vilene mask. Pin and tack down dart and smooth out face, matching all edges. Pin and tack all layers together. Topstitch 3 mm (1/8 in) round complete mask shape. Remove all tacking.

10 Tack through all mask layers at eye hole. Either zig-zag or oversew edges to neaten. Cut round bottom half of eye hole through all layers. Fringe top half on both felt layers. Cut away vilene and wadding completely.

11 Position 'woolly fringe' as photograph. Pin and catchstitch to top of head.

KOALA

materials

60 cm (23½ in) square silver grey felt
22 cm (8½ in) square coral pink felt
30 cm (11¾ in) of 82 cm (32¼ in)-wide craft-quality vilene
20 cm (8 in) of 1 m (39½ in)-wide lightweight polyester wadding
8 cm (3 in) of 2 cm (¾ in)-wide light grey velcro
1 black plastic oval nose, 4 cm (1½ in) long
matching thread (grey, pink)
centimetre pattern paper
scissors, pencil, tailor's chalk, ruler, fabric adhesive

to make

1 Transfer the diagrams to centimetre pattern paper. Using these as the patterns, cut the following:
from grey felt 2 mask shapes, 4 cheek shapes, 1 nose shape, 1 chin shape, 2 headband strips 22 cm (8½ in) × 5 cm (2 in)
from pink felt 2 inner ear shapes
from vilene 1 mask shape
from wadding 2 cheek circles, 2 inner ears, 1 nose, 1 chin.

2 Pin and tack the hook and loop pieces of velcro to one end of each headband strip, horizontal to long edges and 1 cm (⅜ in) from short end. Machine stitch. Remove tacking.

3 Pin, tack and machine stitch centre forehead dart in both grey felt mask shapes and in vilene. Slit and press felt darts open. Trim vilene dart down to 3 mm (1/8 in) turnings. Remove tacking.

4 Matching dart turnings on front felt mask to dart seam on vilene interlining mask, pin and tack through both dart seams. Smooth out mask. Match and pin outer edges together. Position one end of each felt headband piece to sides of mask as diagram, making sure that the hook and loop lengths face in and out and join together at the back of head. Pin and tack.

5 Overlapping 6 mm (¼ in), pin and tack curved mouth edge of felt chin piece to straight edge of felt nose. Match these tacked pieces to the corresponding tacked wadding nose and chin. Pin and tack. Topstitch across mouth curve to create 'smile' on nose and chin.

6 Pin and tack one wadding cheek circle between two grey felt cheek circles. Tucking any visible wadding in from edge, pin, tack and topstitch 3 mm (1/8 in) from edge. Repeat for other cheek. Remove tacking.

7 Pin and tack cheek circles to face as shown on diagram. Topstitch 3 mm (1/8 in) from edge. Remove tacking.

8 Pin and tack the corresponding wadding shapes to the pink felt inner ear pieces. Pin and tack in position on mask shape. Topstitch 3 mm (1/8 in) from edge. Remove tacking.

9 Glue plastic nose in position.

10 With wrong sides facing, pin and tack the second grey felt mask shape to the vilene mask. Smooth out, matching

all edges. Topstitch 3 mm (⅛ in) around complete mask shape.

11 Tack through all three mask layers at eye hole. Zig-zag or oversew edges to neaten. Trim away to make eye hole. Remove all visible tacking.

HARE

materials

60 cm (23½ in) square silver grey felt
22 cm (8½ in) square coral pink felt
22 cm (8½ in) square pale orange felt
22 cm (8½ in) square tangerine felt
22 cm (8½ in) square moss green felt
30 cm (11¾ in) of 82 cm (32¼ in)-wide vilene
35 cm (13¾ in) of 1 m (39½ in)-wide light-weight polyester wadding
8 cm (3 in) of 2 cm (¾ in)-wide grey velcro
matching thread for different felts
centimetre pattern paper
scissors, pencil, tailor's chalk, ruler

to make

1 Transfer the diagrams to centimetre pattern paper. Using these as your patterns, cut the following:
from grey felt 2 mask shapes, 2 headband strips (see page 35)
from pink felt 2 inner ear shapes, 2 nose shapes
from pale orange felt 1 snout shape
from tangerine felt 1 carrot shape
from moss green felt half of the 22 cm (8½ in) square, snipped at intervals of 6 mm (¼ in) almost to end of its 11 cm (4¼ in) width
from vilene 1 mask shape, 1 pair teeth
from wadding 2 snout shapes, 1 mask shape, 1 nose shape, 1 carrot shape, plus scraps to pad carrot.

2 Pin and tack the hook and loop pieces of velcro to one end of each headband strip, horizontal to long edges and 1 cm (⅜ in) from short end. Machine stitch. Remove tacking.

3 Pin, tack and machine stitch the centre forehead dart in both grey felt mask shapes and the vilene interlining. Slit and lightly press felt darts open. Trim vilene dart down to 3 mm (⅛ in) turnings. Remove tacking.

4 Pin and tack the vilene mask shape to the polyester wadding mask shape (there is no need for a dart in the wadding). Pin and tack one felt mask to the wadding mask, wrong side facing the wadding and matching outer edges. Tack headband pieces in position on each side of mask, making sure velcro lengths face each other to join at the back of the head.

5 Sandwich the wadding nose shape between the two pink nose shapes. Pin and tack, tucking in any visible wadding. Topstitch, marking nostril shapes as diagram. Remove tacking.

6 Pin and catchstitch gum edge of teeth under the straight edge of the back of padded nose.

7 Position the pink felt inner ears to the hare as diagram. Pin, tack and topstitch close to the edge. Remove the tacking.

8 Pin and tack the two wadding snout shapes to the pale orange snout shape. Position snout shape on hare's face as diagram. Pin, tack and topstitch close to the edge of orange shape. Remove the tacking.

9 Position pink felt nose on snout as diagram. Pin and catchstitch.

10 With wrong sides facing, match the second felt mask shape to vilene mask. Pin and tack down dart and smooth out face, matching all edges. Pin all four layers together and tack, matching outer edges. Topstitch 3 mm (⅛ in) round complete mask shape. Remove all tacking.

11 Working through all thicknesses, pin and tack round eye shape, avoiding eyelid. Either zig-zag or handsew edges to neaten. Remove tacking. Carefully trim bottom half to form eyelids on front grey mask. Remove vilene, wadding and back grey felt eye to make eyehole.

12 Match the wadding carrot shape to the tangerine felt shape. Pin, tack and topstitch on the marked lines. Roll carrot, overlapping long edges. Pin and catchstitch, working from tip to top. Push scraps of wadding into the carrot to round out the shape. Roll the snipped carrot leaves to form a 'brush' shape and insert into top of the padded carrot. Using tangerine thread, run a line of gathering stitches round the top of the carrot and pull up to secure. Catchstitch carrot to face of hare.

13 Fold left ear as shown and catchstitch in position.

Scale 1 square = 5 cm (approx 2 in)

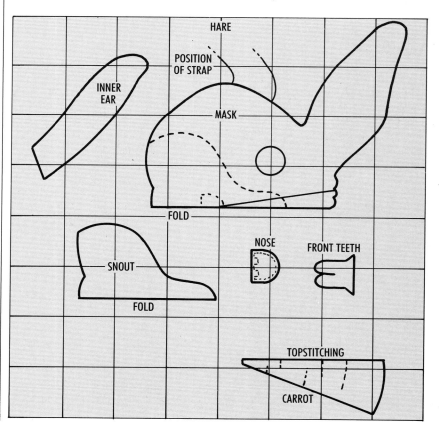

SWIMMING PACK

These practical swimming packs are in fact unisex, but our 'girl's' pack has lots of pockets for carrying brushes, bottles and all the beauty aids that youngsters need. Both packs are made from strong, bright-coloured canvas and lined with waterproof cotton-backed PVC to hold wet swimming togs, damp towels, goggles, etc. The pockets on the 'boy's' pack are sealed with velcro to ensure a safe journey to the swimming baths.

FOR A GIRL

materials

70 cm (27½ in) of 44 cm (17¼ in)-wide yellow deckchair canvas
60 cm (23½ in) of 150 cm (59 in)-wide blue-and-white striped cotton-backed PVC
40 cm (15¾ in) of 1 m (39½ in)-wide light-weight polyester wadding
20 cm (8 in) of 2 cm (¾ in)-wide blue velcro
matching thread (yellow, white)
centimetre pattern paper
scissors, ballpoint pen, pencil, ruler, teflon foot

to make

1 Transfer the diagrams to centimetre pattern paper. Using these as your patterns, cut the following:
from canvas 2 straps, 2 handles cut on dotted line, 1 pack oblong, 1 pocket oblong
from PVC 2 straps, 2 handles cut on dotted line, 1 pack lining oblong, 1 pocket oblong
from polyester wadding 1 pack lining oblong
from velcro 2 × 10 cm (4 in) lengths.
2 On the canvas pack oblong, turn a 1 cm (⅜ in) hem to the wrong side along all four edges. Pin, tack and machine stitch 6 mm (¼ in) from the edge. Turn a 2.5 cm (1 in) hem to the right side on each edge. Holding two corner points together, pin and tack the mitre line. Machine stitch. Remove tacking. Trim the seams down to 6 mm (¼ in). Repeat process for each corner. Turn point of mitred corner out to right side, forming a 'frame' edge for the canvas case of the swimming pack.

3 Tear apart the two 10 cm (4 in) strips of velcro and position each loop half on one end of one canvas strap as shown on the pattern. Pin, tack and machine stitch. Remove tacking. Position the corresponding hook halves of the velcro at one end of each PVC strap on the right side.
4 With right sides together, match the top long edges of the PVC pocket and canvas pocket oblong so that the bottom long edge of the PVC overlaps the

Scale   1 square = 5 cm (approx 2 in)

canvas by 1 cm (⅜ in). Pin, tack and machine-stitch with 1 cm (⅜ in) turnings. Turn the PVC over on to the canvas to form a binding. With wrong sides together, pin and tack with 6 mm (¼ in) turnings down the short sides of the pocket to hold.
5 Attach the pocket to the PVC lining. With the bound edge face down, place the lined pocket length across the width of the PVC lining, matching the notches to the centre notches of the PVC lining. With 1 cm (⅜ in) turning, pin, tack and machine stitch the double pocket oblongs to the PVC lining. Remove tacking. Turn pocket over on to the left side, PVC pocket lining to pack lining.

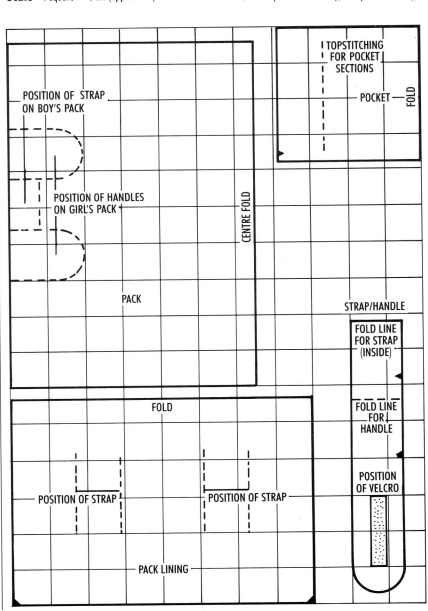

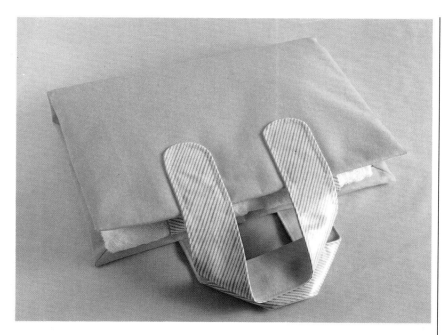

Smooth pocket shape flat. Pin and tack the short sides of the pocket to the pack lining.

6 To form sections in the pocket, at approximately 13 cm (5 in) intervals, pin, tack and topstitch a single line twice, working from the bound top to the canvas bottom of the lined pocket.

7 Place the strap pieces with right sides together and the velcro pairs inside at opposite ends. With a 6 mm (¼ in) turning and leaving the 15 cm (6 in) opening centrally on one long side of strap, pin, tack and machine stitch the strap pieces together. Remove tacking. Turn the strap to the right side. Repeat for the other strap. Sliding turnings to inside, tack the opening together and pin and tack round the straps. Place tissue paper under the PVC side of the straps and topstitch on the canvas side, approximately 6 mm (¼ in) from the edge. Remove tacking.

8 Make the handles in the same way as the straps.

9 Attach the straps to the PVC lining. With the PVC lining facing the PVC side of the straps, position the straps to the right of the pocket (see dotted 'H's), at a point approximately 16 cm (6¼ in) in from the right-hand short side. The straps should be parallel to the long sides of lining with a gap of 11 cm (4¼ in) between them. Pin, tack and machine stitch an oblong 4 cm (1½ in) × 1 cm (⅜ in) across the centre of the straps to hold them in place. Remove

tacking.

10 Attach the handles to the canvas case. With a gap of approximately 7 cm (2¾ in) between the ends of the handles, position centrally, overlapping the curved ends approximately 10 cm (4 in) on the right side of the canvas case. Pin and tack, opening out the canvas frame edge. Topstitch curved ends to within 1 cm (⅜ in) from fold of frame edge. Remove tacking.

11 Place the wadding oblong to the cotton side of the PVC lining. Pin and tack outer edges together. Slide the polyester wadding and PVC lining inside the canvas case. If the lining distorts the case, remove and trim the PVC wadding/lining to fit. Replace inside canvas case. Pin and tack along stitched edge. Catchstitch and remove tacking. Wrap the straps around a towel, matching the halves of the velcro.

FOR A BOY

materials

70 cm (27½ in) of 150 cm (59 in)-wide blue awning canvas
47 cm (18½ in) of 150 cm (59 in)-wide yellow cotton-backed PVC
27 cm (10½ in) of 150 cm (59 in)-wide blue cotton-backed PVC
scraps of contrasting PVC (pockets)
35 cm (13¾ in) of 1 m (39½ in)-wide white plastic lining
40 cm (15¾ in) of 1 m (39½ in)-wide light-weight polyester wadding
26 cm (10¼ in) of 2 cm (¾ in)-wide sky blue velcro
matching thread (light blue, dark blue)
centimetre pattern paper
fabric adhesive, scissors, ballpoint pen, ruler, teflon foot

to make

1 Transfer the diagrams to the centimetre pattern paper. Using these as your pattern, cut the following:
from blue awning canvas 1 oblong 66 cm (26 in) × 46 cm (18 in) for the outer casing
from yellow cotton-backed PVC 1 oblong 57 cm (22½ in) × 38 cm (15 in) for the lining, 1 strap
from blue cotton-backed PVC 1 oblong 57 cm (22½ in) × 20 cm (8 in) for the large pocket, 1 strap, bird shape
from contrasting scraps of cotton-backed PVC 2 pockets
from white plastic 1 oblong 57 cm (22½ in) × 22 cm (8½ in) for the pocket top binding; 57 cm (22½ in) × 8 cm (3¼ in) for pocket base binding; 2 oblong strips 22 cm (8½ in) × 8 cm (3¼ in) for pocket side bindings
from polyester wadding 1 oblong 57 cm (22½ in) × 38 cm (15 in)
from velcro 2 strips each 7 cm (2¾ in) long and 2 strips each 6 cm (2⅜ in) long.

2 To attach the velcro to the two small pockets, tear apart the 6 cm (2⅜ in) velcro hook and loop pieces. Position each hook piece as shown on the pattern on the inner right side of the pocket strip. Pin, tack and machine stitch. Remove tacking. Fold the pocket strip in half lengthways, wrong sides facing, and match the curved ends

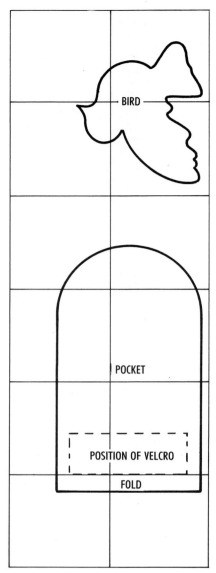

Scale 1 square = 5 cm (approx 2 in)

WORKING WITH PVC

Working with PVC can prove difficult. The cotton side will run through the machine easily, but the plastic side may stick under the machine foot. Use a teflon foot or roller foot if possible, or place a layer of tissue paper over the plastic surface and stitch over the tissue, which can be torn away from the stitch line when finished. Secure hems with sellotape, but remove it completely as soon as the hem has been stitched.

exactly. Position each loop half of the 6 cm (2⅜ in) velcro strips to the PVC side of the blue pocket (see diagram). Pin, tack and machine stitch. Remove tacking.

3 To attach the pockets to the blue PVC pocket oblong, match the velcro hook and loop pieces. Pin, tack and machine-topstitch around the pockets 3 mm (⅛ in) from the edge, leaving the top of the pocket open. Remove the tacking stitches.

4 Join the white plastic side bindings to the blue PVC pocket. With right sides together position one long side of each 22 cm (8½ in) strip to each short side of the blue PVC pocket. Matching raw edges, pin, tack and machine stitch down centre of each 8 cm (3¼ in) width. Remove tacking. Fold on the machined line, bringing the wrong sides together. Pin and tack.

5 Line the blue PVC pocket oblong with white plastic. With the right side of the white plastic pocket oblong to the right side of the blue PVC oblong and over bound side seams, pin, tack and machine stitch with a 1 cm (⅜ in) turning across the top edge. Remove tacking. Turn the white plastic lining over the 1 cm (⅜ in) turning, matching the wrong sides. Smooth the lining flat down the back of the pocket. Pin and tack to hold in place.

6 Join the base binding strip of white plastic to the blue PVC pocket. With right sides together position the long side of the 57 cm (22½ in) strip to the base edge of the PVC pocket. Matching raw edges, pin, tack and machine stitch along centre of the 8 cm (3¼ in) width. Remove tacking. Trim away excess thicknesses at corners. Fold on the machined line, bringing the wrong sides together. Pin and tack.

7 To make the canvas case, turn a 1 cm (⅜ in) hem on all sides of the canvas oblong. Pin, tack and machine stitch. Turn the right side hemmed edge 2.5 cm (1 in) over on to the right side of

the canvas. Pin the corners to form a mitre and press slightly to form a crease. Pin, tack and machine stitch. Trim the corner seams down to 6 mm (¼ in). Remove the tacking stitches and press open. Repeat for each corner. Turn the corners to the right side, pushing the points out. Press again.

8 Pin, tack and topstitch two vertical lines 14 cm (5½ in) and 26 cm (10¼ in) from left side of bound pocket. Remove tacking.

9 To make the strap, arrange the loop halves of the 7 cm (2¾ in) strips of velcro on the rounded end and centre of blue strap, lengthways. Arrange the corresponding hook halves on the yellow strap (see diagram). Place the right side of the yellow PVC strap with the velcro strips at opposite ends. With a 6 mm (¼ in) turning, pin, tack and machine stitch, leaving a 20 cm (8 in) opening between the notches. Snip into the curved ends. Pull the strap through the opening to the right side. Work the strap flat with your hands. Pin and tack to close the opening, tucking in the turnings. Topstitch all around, 3 mm (⅛ in) from the edges. Remove tacking. Secure the strap to the centre of the canvas casing with two vertical lines of machine stitching. Loop strap back to keep it clear while you topstitch canvas case.

10 To assemble the pack, slide the lining into the canvas case and pin and tack along the inner edges. Topstitch 2 mm (¹⁄₁₆ in) from the turned casing edges. Remove all visible tacking.

11 To finish, cover the cotton side of the PVC bird with fabric adhesive and position it on the yellow lining.

Scale 1 square = 5 cm (approx 2 in)

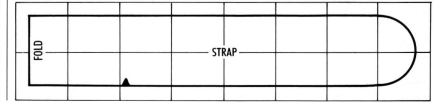

KNITTED HATS

These simple woolly hats are all made from the same basic knitted shape in bright primary colours. Make a different one for each chilly season. The yellow one has a multicoloured pom-pon to brighten up dull autumn days, while spring chicks made from small acrylic pom-pons perch jauntily on top of the blue. For Christmas there is a red hat trimmed with holly leaves.

BASIC HAT

materials for 1 hat

1 × 50 g ball of Aran weight yarn
1 pair of 4½ mm needles (size 8)

to make

Cast on 96 stitches.
Knit 65 rows.

Decrease for crown shaping
Row 1 *Knit 7 sts. Knit 2 tog.*
Continue from * to * to end of row.
Row 2 Purl.
Row 3 Knit.
Row 4 Purl.
Row 5 *Knit 6 sts. Knit 2 tog.*
Continue from * to * to end of row.
Decrease in this manner until 12 sts remain on needle. Break off yarn and pull through stitches. Draw up tightly and fasten off. Stitch seam. Roll up edge to form brim. Catchstitch to seam.

YELLOW HAT

materials for decoration

lengths of green/red/yellow 4-ply yarn for 8 cm (3 in) diameter pom-pon
2 × 11.5 cm (4⅜ in) squares of cardboard
scissors, pencil, a pair of compasses

to make

1 To make an 8 cm (3 in) diameter pom-pon, cut two circles from the card, each 11.25 cm (4⅜ in) in diameter. Remove a 4 cm (1½ in) diameter hole from the centre of both circles. Slit through both circles to form an opening for wool to pass through easily.
2 Bind the wool firmly round the circles, passing through the opening each time. With a continual winding action, build up until the centre hole is filled.
3 Slide one blade of the scissors between the card circles and cut through all wrapped wool.
4 Place two lengths of wool between card circles and tie tufts of pom-pon together firmly, leaving a long end to use for attaching the pom-pon to the hat.
5 Pull the card circles apart and fluff up the strands of the wool.
6 Trim off odd lengths of yarn to form a smooth ball shape.
7 Sew pom-pon to crown using the long length of wool. Catchstitch to secure.

RED HAT

materials for decoration

holly green 4-ply yarn
22 cm (8½ in) square dark green felt
22 cm (8½ in) square scarlet red felt
2 large beads, approximately 2 cm (¾ in) diameter
red thread, scissors, paper, tailor's chalk

to knit holly leaves

Cast on 2 sts.
Increase 1 st at each end of every row, until 20 sts are on the needle.
Decrease 1 st on every row at each end until 12 sts remain.
Increase 1 st at each end of every row back to 20 sts.
Decrease 1 st on every row at each end until 2 sts remain.
Cast off. Repeat for second leaf.

to make

1 To make a pattern for the leaves, pin knitted leaves to paper and draw outline. Using pattern and chalk, mark and cut out two green felt holly leaves.
Cut two 6 cm (2⅜ in) circles from the red felt square.
2 Place knitted leaf on felt leaf and

catchstitch to secure. Fold each leaf across centre, matching leaf outlines. Catchstitch together and gather bottom of leaf.
3 Work a line of running stitch 1 cm (⅜ in) inside circles of red felt. Place a bead in the centre and pull up thread to cover. Secure by stitching through felt. Trim raw edges to neaten.
4 Arrange leaves and covered bead berries on top of hat in centre and catchstitch in position.

BLUE HAT

materials for decoration

6 × 3 cm (1¼ in)-diameter yellow acrylic pom-pons
6 × 2 cm (¾ in)-diameter yellow acrylic pom-pons
small pieces of orange and yellow felt
yellow thread, scissors

to make

1 Pass needle and thread through one large and one small pom-pon to form each chick and secure.
2 Cut tiny triangles from orange felt to form beak shapes. Cut slightly larger triangles in yellow felt and catchstitch two to bottom of each chick for feet.
3 Catchstitch base of each large pom-pon to blue knitted hat.

DOG PYJAMA CASE

This cheeky black and white mongrel sits on a black-and-white spotted pyjama case, keeping the contents safe during the day. The dog pieces are 'bagged out' by cutting each piece twice, sewing them together and turning them through. Then they are topstitched to the spotted case front to make this striking present. The lead and the collar can be made from any bright remnants of fabric.

materials

50 cm (20 in) of 90 cm (36 in)-wide black-and-white spotted polyester/cotton fabric

50 cm (20 in) of 136 cm (54 in)-wide black glazed cotton

40 cm (15¾ in) of 136 cm (54 in)-wide white glazed cotton

scraps of red chintz or polyester cotton fabric

50 cm (20 in) of 82 cm (32¼ in)-wide craft-quality vilene

31 cm (12 in) of 2 cm (¾ in)-wide black velcro

matching thread (black, white, red)

1 chrome buckle loop

2 cm (¾ in) joggle eye

adhesive, tailor's chalk, scissors, ballpoint pen, ruler

to make

1 Transfer the diagrams to centimetre pattern paper. Using these as your pattern, cut out the following:

from spotted fabric 1 oblong, measuring 50 × 46 cm (20 × 18 in)

from black glazed cotton 1 left body patch, 1 right body patch, 1 left eye patch, 1 right eye patch, 2 pieces for the back of the case

from white glazed cotton 1 left body, 1 right body, 2 ears

from red fabric 1 left lead, 1 right lead, 1 left collar, 1 right collar.

2 Place the two white body shapes right sides together. Pin, tack and machine stitch them with 6 mm (¼ in) turnings, leaving the seam open between the notches. Remove the tacking. Snip into the curves or angles around the edge.

3 Make the ear, body patch and eye patch in the same way as the body shape.

4 Make lead and collar the same way..

5 Remove all tacking. Turn them through to the right side, rolling out and flattening the seams. Pin and tack, tucking in turnings at notched openings.

6 Take a row of tacking around the edge of the dog 5 mm (³⁄₁₆ in) from the edge to hold the shape flat.

7 On the straight open ends of the ear, turn 6 mm (¼ in) to the inside and catchstitch to close. With ear lobe uppermost, catchstitch on line indicated in diagram 1 cm (⅜ in) from raw edge. Allow the ear to flop down.

8 Pin and tack the body patch and eye patch to the dog 6 mm (¼ in) from the edges to hold them flat (see diagram). Topstitch in black 3 mm (⅛ in) from the edges.

9 Place the collar in position and pin and tack 6 mm (¼ in) from the edges. Topstitch in red 3 mm (⅛ in) from the edge.

10 Pin and tack the dog on the spotted fabric oblong. Using white thread, topstitch all around 3 mm (⅛ in) from the edge. Mark the front legs as shown in diagram. Remove all of the tacking stitches.

11 Fold 2 cm (¾ in) of the lead over the buckle bar and catchstitch it invis-

BAGGING OUT

Bagging out is handy when a sharply turned shape is needed. Two facing pieces are cut, pinned, tacked and machine stitched with very narrow turnings. Leave an opening on a straight edge. Trim the seam allowances and snip any curves. Turn 'shape' to right side and roll out the stitched edge between the thumb and fingers. Catchstitch the opening to close, tack piece flat and press. Pin, tack and topstitch to finish.

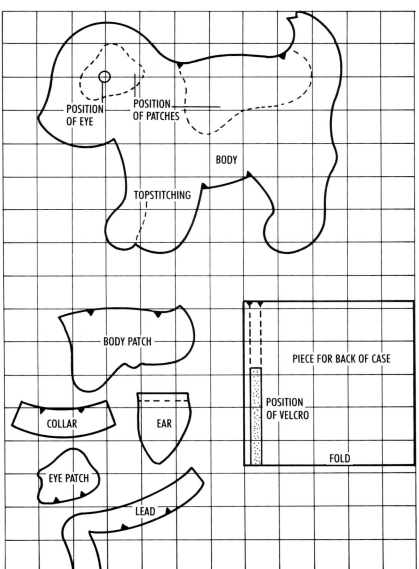

POSITION OF EYE
POSITION OF PATCHES
BODY
TOPSTITCHING
BODY PATCH
COLLAR
EAR
PIECE FOR BACK OF CASE
POSITION OF VELCRO
FOLD
EYE PATCH
LEAD

Scale 1 square = 5 cm (approx 2 in)

ibly to the wrong side. Secure the lead to the top of the collar with oversewing and arrange as in photograph. Pin, tack and topstitch with red thread 3 mm (⅛ in) from the edge. Remove tacking.

12 Pin and tack the vilene to the wrong side of the black-and-white spotted fabric oblong.

13 Make a 1 cm (⅜ in) hem on one long side of each black oblong on the wrong side. Pin, tack and machine stitch. Remove tacking and press. Pull apart the 31 cm (12 in) length of black velcro and position the hook and velcro pieces centrally on the right side of each black oblong (see diagram). Pin, tack and machine stitch. Remove tacking. Turn a further 2 cm (¾ in) on one oblong with velcro to the wrong side. Pin and tack the sides to hold them firmly in place.

14 To make the case, join the hook and loop velcro strips to form a complete back. With the right sides of the back and spotted front together and the edges matching, pin, tack and machine stitch with 6 mm (¼ in) turnings. Remove the tacking stitches. Tear apart the velcro and turn the oblong through to the right side.

15 Apply adhesive to the back of joggle eye and to the marked circle on the patch. Allow this to become tacky, then glue the eye in position.

MESSENGER BIRDS

These birds are cut from pretty pastel shades of felt and stitched to a base of craft-quality vilene. They perch on wooden rods that stand in a firm wooden base. Make each bird unique by coming up with your own colour scheme and write a message on the label around each bird's neck.

LONG BIRD

materials for 1 bird

15 cm (6 in) of 82 cm (32¼ in)-wide craft-quality vilene

31 cm (12 in) square felt for main body

2 × 22 cm (8½ in) square felt in contrasting colours

matching thread for different colours of felt

2 small beads

centimetre paper

fabric adhesive, ballpoint pen

25 cm (10 in) length of 1 cm (⅜ in) square wooden rod

25 cm (10 in) × 4.5 cm (1¾ in) strip of felt (for rod)

wooden base: block of sanded wood 10 cm (4 in) wide × 8 cm (3 in) deep × 5 cm (2 in) high

hammer and chisel

wood adhesive

thin card 5 cm (2 in) × 8 cm (3 in)

hole punch

thin cord

Scale 1 square = 5 cm (approx 2 in)

to make

Transfer the diagrams for the long bird to the centimetre pattern paper and cut the following:

from vilene 1 body

from felt 2 bodies, 2 wings, 2 tails, 2 heads, 2 eye outlines, 2 beaks, 12 triangles (for decoration), 2 oblongs 5 cm (2 in) × 8 cm (3 in), 2 oblongs 5 cm (2 in) × 10 cm (4 in), 1 oblong 8 cm (3 in) × 10 cm (4 in), 1 oblong 5 cm (2 in) × 8 cm (3 in) for backing card.

1 Assemble bird as in the diagram, pinning and tacking felt pieces to one side of the vilene body in the following order: one body, one wing, one tail, one head and one beak.

2 Using matching thread, topstitch 3 mm (⅛ in) round all edges, leaving a 2 cm (¾ in) opening at base of bird. If

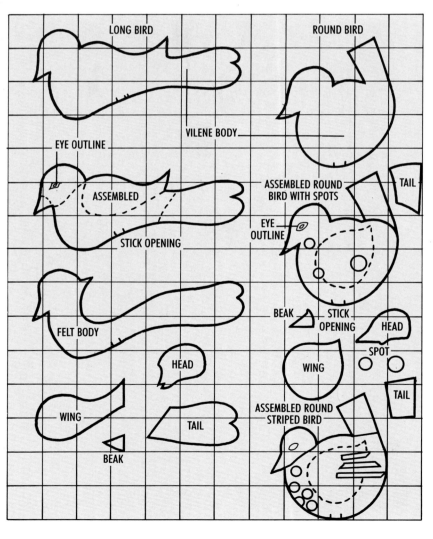

your machine will not take these thicknesses, either catchstitch the pieces together or use fabric adhesive.

3 Using fabric adhesive, position the eye outlines and sew beads to centres.

4 Position the triangles using fabric adhesive.

Repeat for other side of bird.

5 Cover the wooden rod with a thin coat of fabric adhesive. Allow to become tacky. Smooth a felt strip on to the rod, applying pressure to the four sides by rolling slowly on a flat surface. Catchstitch the overlapping long edge to neaten.

6 Using a hammer and chisel, make a 1 cm (⅜ in) square hole in the centre of one flat side of the wooden base.

7 Cover the side with the hole in it and the corresponding large oblong of felt with fabric adhesive. Allow to become tacky and fuse to top of block. Repeat for side oblongs. When adhesive is dry, carefully cut out a square hole in felt to correspond with hole in block.

8 Partly fill the square hole in the top of the block with wood adhesive, then slide the felt-covered rod into hole.

9 Push top end of the felt-covered rod into base of bird's body. Catchstitch the base of bird together around the felt-covered rod.

10 To make the card tag, cover an oblong of card with a matching felt oblong using fabric adhesive. Round off corners neatly and fold the card in half widthways. Punch a hole in the top just next to the fold. Loop a length of thin cord through and tie it. Slide over the bird's head.

ROUND BIRD

materials for 1 bird

20 cm (8 in) of 82 cm (32¼ in)-wide craft-quality vilene
2 × 22 cm (8½ in) square of felt in same colour for main body
3 × 22 cm (8½ in) square of felt in contrasting colours
matching thread
2 small beads
centimetre paper
fabric adhesive, ballpoint pen
25 cm (10 in) length of 1 cm (⅜ in) square wooden rod
25 cm (10 in) × 4.5 cm (1¾ in) strip of felt (for rod)
wooden base: block of sanded wood 10 cm (4 in) wide × 8 cm (3 in) deep × 5 cm (2 in) high
hammer and chisel
wood adhesive
thin card 5 cm (2 in) × 8 cm (3 in)
hole punch
thin cord

to make

Transfer the diagrams for the round bird to the centimetre pattern paper and cut the following:

from vilene 1 body
from felt 2 bodies, 2 wings, 2 tails, 2 heads, 2 eye outlines, 2 beaks, small circles and stripes (see photograph) for decoration, 2 oblongs 5 cm (2 in) × 8 cm (3 in), 2 oblongs 5 cm (2 in) × 10 cm (4 in), 1 oblong 8 cm (3 in) × 10 cm (4 in), 1 oblong 5 cm (2 in) × 8 cm (3 in).

Assemble as for long bird, following Steps 1-10, but in Step 4 decorate with circles and stripes instead of triangles.

USING ADHESIVES

Different types of glue are used for the projects in this book. A spirit/petrol-based adhesive is ideal for sticking fabrics together, as it doesn't mark. If handling polystyrene, apply a water-based adhesive. And when binding pieces of wood together, a wood adhesive is the best choice as it is very strong.

TEENAGERS' BIRTHDAYS

Teenagers can be difficult to please on their birthdays – records, tapes and clothes often seem to be the only presents greeted with any enthusiasm by this age group. With a little ingenuity, however, it is possible to come up with gifts that will be appreciated. Generally, anything connected with vanity or their bedrooms, the retreat away from the adult world, goes down well.

An evening bag made from silver and pale pink printed lamé would be welcomed by most teenage girls. Three different patterns are given so you could make a set. Then the ones she doesn't take with her in the evening can be used to keep hair accessories and make-up together. For a boy, make a smart black and white ticking travel roll, lined with black PVC. It will carry a tooth brush, tooth paste, comb, flannel, soap and shaving kit, if he's reached that stage! The mobile (doves suspended on jade coloured satin ribbons) is simple to put together and will cheer up a dark corner of a bedroom. Slightly more challenging would be the Scottie dog set: a piped black and white gingham cushion, and a coat hangar both decorated with small Scottie dogs. Left-over gingham could be used to make a pair of matching slippers, finished off with bright red pom-pons. And the rainbow slippers – made from multi-coloured mohair – make a glamorous, frivolous present for a girl.

in this chapter

- Lamé evening bags
- Scottie dog set
- Boy's travel roll
- Metallic bird mobile
- Rainbow slippers

Right Many of the presents have already been put to use in this teenager's attic bedroom. A metallic bird mobile hangs from the corner and a gingham cushion, part of the Scottie dog set, has found a home on the bed. The proud receiver of the rainbow slippers couldn't resist trying them on, while she examined one of the evening lamé bags. Her brother is pre-occupied with the smart black and white ticking travel roll.
Left A detail of an evening lamé bag showing the tassel decoration and quilting.

LAMÉ EVENING BAGS

These little pink and silver clutch bags in shining lamé are perfect for evening parties, and they also make wonderfully elegant make-up bags for a teenage girl. They are made from circles of plain or printed lamé lined with lightweight polyester wadding and vilene and bound with matching lamé bias binding. Tassels and decorative top-stitching provide the finishing touches.

SMALL BAG

materials

19 cm (7½ in) round plate
20 cm (8 in) square of white paper
25 cm (10 in) of 115 cm (45 in)-wide pale pink lamé
2 × 25 cm (10 in) squares printed pink-on-silver lamé
25 cm (10 in) square craft-quality vilene
25 cm (10 in) square lightweight polyester wadding
matching thread (pink)
1 silver press fastener
bondaweb
scissors, pencil

to make

1 Place the plate on the white paper and draw around it to make a circle. Cut out the circle, and using it as your pattern, cut the following:
from plain lamé 2 circles, 2 oblongs, each 16 cm (6¼ in) × 8 cm (3 in) for tassel
from printed lamé 2 circles
from vilene 1 circle
from wadding 1 circle.

2 From remaining plain lamé, cut out bias lengths each measuring 5 cm (2 in) wide (see page 52). Join them on the straight edge to form a bias strip measuring 60 cm (23½ in) × 5 cm (2 in).

3 Pin and tack the vilene and wadding circles together. Sandwich between the wrong sides of one printed and one plain lamé circle. Pin and tack.

4 To achieve a quilted look, topstitch at 1 cm (⅜ in) intervals across half of the lamé/wadding/vilene circles (see the photograph).

5 To make pockets, fold the two remaining circles – one printed, one plain – in half, wrong sides together. Tack round the curved edges. Position one half of the press fastener centrally 3 cm (1¼ in) from the centre fold on one printed lamé circle and sew in place.

6 With the folded edges of the pockets running parallel to each other, place each one on its matching side of the quilted circle. Pin and tack 6 mm (¼ in) from the edge of the circle.

7 Press the long edges of the bias strip into the centre, forming folds of 1.2 cm (½ in). Open out *one* folded side of the strip and, matching the raw edge to the raw edge of the lamé bag circle, pin,

tack and machine stitch on the 1.2 cm (½ in) crease. Wrap the other folded side of the bias over the bag shape. Pin, tack and catchstitch the crease to lamé circle. Neaten the end of the binding by overlapping and turning a 2 mm (¹⁄₁₆ in) hem on the straight grain.

8 To make a tassel, place the adhesive side of the bondaweb to the wrong side of the lamé tassel oblong. Press with a warm dry iron. Peel off the paper and fuse the second oblong to other side of bondaweb. Trim 2 mm (¹⁄₁₆ in) from the edges to neaten the shape. At intervals of 6 mm (¼ in), snip along one long edge of the lamé oblong to a depth of 5 cm (2 in) to form fringing. Roll up the oblong to form a tassel and catchstitch the end of the unfringed section to hold the tassel in place.

9 Catchstitch the tassel to the bias binding at outside centre of bag flap.

10 Position the second half of the press fastener on the inside flap behind the tassel to match the half on the pocket. Sew in place. Do not take the stitches through to the front of the flap.

LARGE PINK BAG

materials

23 cm (9 in) plate
25 cm (10 in) square of white paper
25 cm (10 in) of 115 cm (45 in)-wide pale pink lamé
2 × 25 cm (10 in) squares printed pink-on-silver lamé
2 × 25 cm (10 in) squares craft-quality vilene
2 × 25 cm (10 in) squares lightweight polyester wadding
matching thread (pink)
20 cm (8 in) strip of 9 cm (3½ in)-wide bondaweb
1 silver press fastener
scissors, pencil

to make

1 Transfer the plate shape to the white paper. Using this as your pattern, cut the following:
from plain lamé 2 circles, 2 oblongs 20 cm (8 in) × 9 cm (3½ in), bias lengths joined on the straight grain to form three bias strips each 35 cm (13¾ in) × 5 cm (2 in) (see small bag, Step 2)
from printed lamé 3 circles
from vilene 2 circles
from wadding 2 circles.

2 Pin and tack one vilene and one wadding circle together. Repeat to make a second circle. Match wadding side to wrong side of one printed lamé circle and vilene side to wrong side of one plain lamé circle. Pin and tack to hold. Pin and tack.

3 Fold remaining printed circle in half, wrong sides together, for pocket. Matching weave of lamé, position pocket on one printed/padded circle.

4 Cover top edge of half of each complete circle with a 35 cm (13¾ in) bias strip, as small bag, Step 7. Begin and end bias strip above pocket on printed side. Pin, tack and topstitch, but do not neaten ends. Remove tacking.

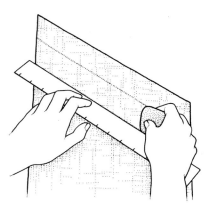

1 To make bias binding strips, find the true bias grain of the fabric by folding it diagonally. Using a ruler and tailor's chalk, mark 5 cm (2 in) strips and then cut out.

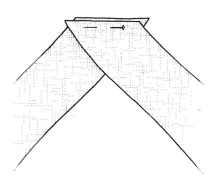

2 To join the bias strips, place the ends right sides together. Pin, tack and stitch along the straight grain with 6 mm (¼ in) turnings. Press the seams open.

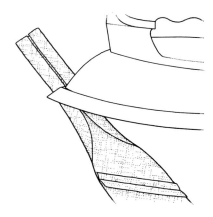

3 Press both long edges to the centre, wrong sides inside, to form 1.2 cm (½ in) creases on the 2.5 cm (1 in) finished width. The bias binding is ready for use.

5 With pink lamé circles together and bound halves at the top, pin and tack 6 mm (¼ in) from bottom raw edges. Bind bottom edges as small bag, turning a 6 mm (¼ in) hem on the straight grain to neaten (see small bag, Step 7). Remove tacking.

6 Make tassel and attach as small bag (Step 8). Position as photograph.

7 Sew one half of the press fastener behind the tassel and match the other half on the printed pocket, approximately 5 cm (2 in) from bottom edge of the bag. Sew in place securely.

SILVER LAMÉ BAG

materials

20 cm (8 in) plate
25 cm (10 in) square of white paper
50 cm (20 in) of 115 cm (45 in)-wide silver lamé
25 cm (10 in) square craft-quality vilene
2 × 25 cm (10 in) squares lightweight polyester wadding
matching thread (silver grey)
1 silver press fastener
scissors, pencil, ruler, quilting pen

to make

1 Transfer the plate shape to the white paper. Using this as your pattern, cut the following:

from silver lamé 4 circles, bias lengths joined on the straight grain to form one continuous bias strip 109 cm (43 in) × 5 cm (2 in) long
from vilene 1 circle
from wadding 2 circles.

2 Pin and tack one wadding circle to wrong side of one lamé circle. Run lines of tacking stitches to form an 'X' across circle to hold lamé firm.

3 Mark tiny dots on the padded lamé circle in the following positions, using ruler and quilting pen. Mark a point 8.5 cm (3¼ in) from raw edge towards centre of circle. Make an upturned 'V' by flaring approximately 7 cm (2¾ in) on either side of this central line. Continue to mark at 6 mm (¼ in) intervals down to raw edges until the last upturned 'V' measures 1.2 cm (½ in) deep.

Run lines of tacking between the dotted lines to stop a 'dragging' effect on fabric. Topstitch on marked lines. Remove tacking.

QUILTING

Padding with polyester wadding and then topstitching your fabric will create a quilting effect. Marking the quilting lines can be difficult so use a felt tip pen and a long tacking stitch. Start tacking from the centre, smoothing outwards as you go.

4 With chevron side of lamé circle to right side of one lamé circle, pin and tack half of the circle with 1 cm (⅜ in) turnings. Position chevron side centrally in this stitched half circle. Machine stitch. Trim stitched turnings down to 6 mm (¼ in). Remove tacking. Turn through to right side. Tack machined half to hold firm.

5 Fold one single-layer lamé circle in half and sew on one half of the press fastener centrally 2 cm (¾ in) from the fold.

6 Matching all curved edges and with the press fastener showing, position the pocket on the plain lamé side of the padded chevron-stitched circles. Pin and tack.

7 Pin and tack vilene circle to wadding circle. Sandwich this between wrong sides of the two remaining lamé circles. Pin and tack. Place the chevron stitched side to the padded lamé side of this circle. Pin and tack all the layers together.

8 Pin centre of open bias strip to centre base of bag and catchstitch. Bind bag all around the edge by handsewing all layers together or pin, tack and machine stitch very close to long edge and across short ends. Where binding meets on the circles (see photograph), leave ends free but close binding with topstitching to make silver ties. Remove tacking. Tie a bow and catchstitch to hold. Sew second half of press fastener in position to match its partner. Make sure you do not take your stitches through to the front of the flap.

SCOTTIE DOG SET

This selection of three co-ordinated gifts is perfect for the dog-loving teenager. Each piece is made in stylish black-and-white gingham trimmed with accents of red and decorated with bonnie wee Scottie dogs. The padded coat hanger will encourage even the messiest to put away their clothes before settling down comfortably on their new cushion wearing their new slippers.

Of course, you could make the cushion, coat hanger and slippers using a different material and motif.

COAT HANGER

materials

- 25 cm (10 in) of 115 cm (45 in)-wide black-and-white gingham
- 25 cm (10 in) of 115 cm (45 in)-wide white polyester lining
- 1 m (39½ in) of 1 m (39½ in)-wide lightweight polyester wadding
- 43 cm (17 in)-wide wooden coat hanger
- 3 m (3⅓ yd) of 3 mm (⅛ in)-wide red double satin ribbon
- bondaweb
- 6 oblongs 14 cm (5½ in) × 10 cm (4 in) of various black and white polyester/cotton prints
- centimetre pattern paper
- 14 cm (5½ in) × 10 cm (4 in) piece of card
- scissors, tailor's chalk, pencil

to make

1 Transfer the diagrams to the centimetre pattern paper and the dog pattern to the piece of card. Using these as your patterns, cut the following:
from gingham 4 hanger shapes, 1 hook casing 14 cm (5½ in) × 4 cm (1½ in)
from lining 4 hanger shapes
from wadding 4 hanger shapes, 6 strips 1 m (39½ in) × 8 cm (3 in), 4 rounded ends, 1 hook binding 20 cm (8 in) × 3 cm (1¼ in)
from ribbon 1 × 22 cm (8½ in) length (for pulling rouleau through), 3 varying lengths from remaining 2.78 m (3 yd).

2 Fuse bondaweb to the wrong sides of the various print oblongs. Using the card pattern and the pencil, mark three

dog shapes. Cut out. Fuse the dog shapes to the wrong side of each matching oblong. Trim dog shape to give clean edge.

3 To bind the wooden hanger, you need three 1 m (39½ in) strips of wadding for each side. Place the first strip under the base of the metal hook and secure with tacking stitches. Binding firmly, wrap one half of the hanger, working to outer end and back to hook. Secure with tacking stitches. Repeat with two remaining strips. Repeat for other half of hanger.

4 Handstitch two of the four rounded ends of wadding together. Slide over bound ends to give extra padding to the finished hanger.

5 Sandwich a wadding hanger shape between the lining and the wrong side

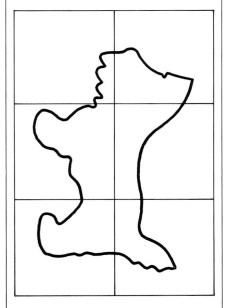

Scale   1 square = 5 cm (approx 2 in)

Scale   1 square = 5 cm (approx 2 in)

of a gingham piece. Pin and tack. Repeat for remaining three sets.

6 Join the gingham/wadding/lining pieces by placing the right sides of gingham together. Pin, tack and machine stitch, using a small zig-zag stitch. Remove tacking. At the end of each oblong case, turn a 1 cm (⅜ in) hem to the lining side. Catchstitch to the lining.

7 Secure the end of the hook binding wadding strip to bound hanger. Secure with tacking stitches. Work up hook, binding firmly, return to base of hook and secure.

8 With right sides together, fold the gingham hook casing in half lengthways, wrapping the 22 cm (8½ in) length of ribbon in fold. Pin, tack and machine stitch across the short end to secure ribbon and continue stitching the long edge 1 cm (⅜ in) from fold, avoiding ribbon.

9 Trim short end down to stitching. Trim long side down to 3 mm (⅛ in). Hold short end firmly with one hand and pull rouleau through. Trim ribbon off close to short end stitches. Slide casing over padded hook. Catchstitch to bound hanger.

10 With a good length of double thread in your needle, handsew a line from the point of the hook, through the gathered fabric casing and secure at the base of the hook. This will stop the gathered casing from falling off the hook.

11 With each cover turned halfway to the right side, slide ends over the well-padded hanger. Turn the remaining gingham cover to right side up to hook. Catchstitch the hemmed edges of the gingham cases together at base of hook.

12 Tie the varying lengths of ribbon round each dog's neck to form a bow or knot. Catchstitch the back centre body of each Scottie dog to the front of the covered hanger (see the photograph for positioning).

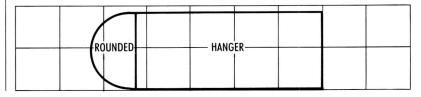

ROUNDED   HANGER

CUSHION

materials

80 cm (31½ in) of 115 cm (45 in)-wide black-and-white gingham
matching thread (black, white)
bondaweb
8 oblongs 14 cm (5½ in) × 10 cm (4 in) of various black and white polyester/cotton prints
2 m (2¼ yd) of 3 mm (⅛ in)-wide red ribbon
31 cm (12 in) of 1.5 cm (⅝ in)-wide black velcro
2 m (2¼ yd) no. 5 cotton piping cord, boiled and dried to avoid shrinkage
31 cm (12 in) black or white zip
40 cm (15¾ in) square feather cushion pad
centimetre pattern paper
14 cm (5½ in) square of card
scissors, ballpoint pen, tailor's chalk, zipper foot

to make

1 Cut 2 squares, each 40 cm (15¾ in), from the gingham.
2 From the remaining gingham, make bias binding. Fold down a corner of the gingham at right angles and press this line. Unfold the fabric and, using tailor's chalk, mark bias strips 4 cm (1½ in) wide parallel to the fold line. Cut out the strips. Pin them together along the straight grain of the short edges, tack and machine stitch with 6 mm (¼ in) turnings. Remove tacking. Press seams.
3 Transfer the Scottie dog diagram to centimetre pattern paper and then to the card. Cut out the shape and use this as your pattern.
4 Fuse bondaweb to wrong side of the assorted black and white fabric remnants by pressing with a warm dry iron. Using the pattern, mark four left and four right-hand dog shapes with a ballpoint pen on the paper side. Cut out

PIPING ON CUSHIONS

Piping will strengthen the seams on a cushion and give a more finished look. Use a piping cord that is proportionately the right size for your cushion and keep to ones that are 100% cotton. Always dry and boil the cord first so that it will not distort the piping when the cushion is cleaned.

the four pairs of dogs for decoration.
5 From the ribbon, cut four 40 cm (15¾ in) lengths.
6 Stiffen dog shapes by removing paper backs from the Scotties and fusing to join the corresponding pairs. Tie a length of red ribbon around each dog's neck. Arrange the Scotties in a row, overlapping slightly, on the flat side of the loop half of the velcro. Pin and tack them in place as shown in the photograph. Catchstitch to secure.
7 Position the hook half of velcro on one gingham cushion square, 10 cm (4 in) from the edge and parallel to one side. Pin, tack and machine stitch. Remove tacking.
8 To make the piping, wrap the wrong side of the gingham bias around the piping cord (right side out). Pin, tack and machine stitch close to the cord, using a zipper foot. Remove tacking and trim the flat edges of piping to 1 cm (⅜ in).
9 Place the end of the covered piping cord on the front cushion cover at the centre of the bottom edge (opposite side to the velcro). Matching all raw edges, pin and tack the piping to the front cover, snipping the turning on the piping at the corners. Open gingham binding and 'meet' the ends of the piping cord at the starting point. Catchstitch cord to secure. Handsew the binding fabric on the straight grain with 6 mm (¼ in) turnings to re-cover the cord. Machine stitch the piping to the front cover, using the zipper foot.
10 Open the zip. With the right side of the zip to the right side of the piping turnings, position the zip centrally on the front cover over the piping seam. One half of the open zip should hang in towards the centre of the cushion cover. Pin, tack and machine stitch close to the teeth of the zip, using a zipper

foot. Remove all the tacking.
11 Match the back cushion cover to the front, right sides together. Pin, tack and machine stitch with 1 cm (⅜ in) turnings, beginning at one end of the open zip, along the other three sides, and ending at the other end of the zip, pressing the zipper foot as close as possible to the piping.
12 Keeping the zip open, match the second side of the zip to the remaining raw edge of the right side of the back cushion cover. Pin, tack and machine stitch the second side of the zip. Remove tacking. Trim all seams and corners. Turn the cushion cover to the right side through the open zip, pushing out the corners.
13 If the stitching on the piping is visible, turn the cushion back to the wrong side and machine stitch closer to the piping cord. Turn the cover back to the right side, slide the pad through the zip opening and push the filling out at the corners.
14 Join the row of Scotties on the loop half of velcro to the hook half of the velcro strip on the front of the cushion.

SLIPPERS

to make

Make a pair of slippers, following the instructions for the basic slipper pattern on page 130, and using 50 cm (20 in) of 115 cm (45 in)-wide black-and-white polyester/cotton gingham. Decorate the slippers with 4 cm (1½ in)-diameter red woollen pom-pons (see pages 62-3 for making a pom-pon), as shown in the photograph here. Alternatively, adorn each slipper with a small Scottie dog, cut from a scrap of plain red, white or black material.

SCOTTIE DOG SET 55

BOY'S TRAVEL ROLL

Made in crisp black-and-white ticking fabric, this practical hard-wearing travel pack lined with PVC makes an ideal gift for a teenage boy. The mattress ticking is interlined with lightweight polyester wadding and the inside is lined with practical cotton-backed PVC. Kiss-laminated PVC lines the deep inside pocket to provide waterproof protection for washing things. The roll is tied with a strap of matching PVC-lined ticking.

materials

70 cm (27½ in) of 145 cm (57 in)-wide black-and-white mattress ticking

45 cm (17¾ in) of 150 cm (59 in)-wide cotton-backed black PVC

40 cm (15¾ in) of 1 m (39½ in)-wide lightweight polyester wadding

25 cm (10 in) length of 129 cm (51 in)-wide red kiss-laminated PVC

matching thread (black)

centimetre pattern paper

scissors, ruler, pencil, ballpoint pen

to make

1 Transfer the diagram for the strap to the centimetre pattern paper. Using this as your pattern, cut the following:

from mattress ticking 1 oblong 68 cm (26¾ in) × 48 cm (19 in); 1 pocket oblong 60 cm (23½ in) × 20 cm (8 in), 1 strap oblong

from black PVC 1 oblong 60 cm (23½ in) × 41 cm (16 in) (for the case lining), 1 strap oblong

from wadding 1 oblong 60 cm (23½ in) × 41 cm (16 in) (for the case lining)

from laminated PVC, marking with ballpoint pen 1 oblong 60 cm (23½ in) × 23 cm (9 in) (for the pocket).

2 Mark notches on one long side of the ticking pocket 10 cm (4 in), 20 cm (8 in) and 30 cm (11¾ in) from the left-hand short side.

3 Pin and tack the wadding to the cotton side of the black PVC.

4 Place the right side of the laminated PVC to the right side of the ticking pocket. Pin and tack. With 1 cm (⅜ in) turnings, machine stitch across the long side without notches. Remove tacking. Open out the fabric and turn the

laminated PVC so that the wrong sides of the fabrics are together. Form a red band 1 cm (⅜ in) wide along the top edge. Smooth the surface flat. Pin and tack the lined pocket 6 mm (¼ in) round the remaining raw edges.

5 Attach the pocket to the black PVC

lining oblong and wadding. Matching the notched, unbound edge of the pocket to the long bottom edge of the black PVC lining, pin and tack the short ends and the base to hold in place.

6 Working at right angles to the long notched edges of the pocket, pin and tack three vertical lines from the notched points made in Step 2 to the red PVC binding at the top of the pocket. Top-

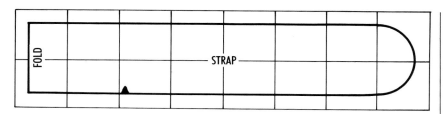

Scale 1 square = 5cm (approx 2in)

stitch in black thread. Remove tacking.

7 Turn a 1cm (⅜in) hem to the wrong side on each side of the ticking oblong. Pin and tack. Turn a 2.5cm (1in) hem to the **right side** on each edge. Grasp the corners, holding the hem points together, and crease a mitre line. Pin and tack on this line. Machine stitch. Remove tacking. Trim the seam down to 6mm (¼in). Press. Repeat for each corner. Turn the point of the corner out to the right side, so that the wrong sides of the ticking are facing and you have formed a frame for the lining of cotton-backed PVC and lightweight polyester wadding.

8 With the PVC and ticking pocket uppermost, slide the pocket into the ticking frame. Smooth the pocket outwards towards each side. If the casing puckers, trim the outer edges of PVC, as the lining must lie flat. Pin, tack and topstitch 2mm (¹⁄₁₆in) from the inner turned edges. Remove any visible tacking.

9 Make the strap. With the right sides of the black PVC and ticking straps together, pin, tack and machine stitch with 6mm (¼in) turnings, beginning and ending at the notched opening. Remove tacking. Snip the curves. Turn the strap through to the right side and roll the edges flat. Pin, tack and topstitch 3mm (⅛in) from the edges.

10 Fold the travel roll in half widthways and tie the strap to hold.

JEWELLERY ROLL

Make a slightly more feminine version of this travel roll for a girl to keep her jewellery in. Choose a bright fabric, like the ice cream coloured cotton print shown here.

METALLIC BIRD MOBILE

A flock of pretty blue and green metallic birds flies out from a circle of card. The birds flutter on lengths of thin satin ribbon in a delicate mobile to decorate a teenager's room.

materials

10 cm (4 in) × 5 cm (2 in) piece of firm white card for bird pattern
20 cm (8 in)-diameter round plate
rubber solution paper adhesive, glue spreader or plastic knife
70 cm (27½ in) × 50 cm (20 in) sheet of metallic blue card
70 cm (27½ in) × 50 cm (20 in) sheet of metallic green card
10 m (11 yd) of 3 mm (⅛ in)-wide jade green double satin ribbon
centimetre pattern paper
sharp pointed scissors, pencil, hole puncher

to make

NOTE When cutting any shape on paper or card, always use the centre of the blade on the scissors; using the points makes a jagged edge.
1 Transfer the diagram to centimetre pattern paper and then to the card. This will give a firmer pattern.
2 Mark a 20 cm (8 in)-diameter circle on the white side of the blue and green sheets of card, using the plate. Cut out the two circles. Using the glue spreader or plastic knife, apply a thin coat of adhesive to both white sides of circles. Leave adhesive to become tacky, then join circles.
3 When glue is dry, using one side of the hole puncher, make 24 evenly spaced holes approximately 2 cm (¾ in) in from the edge of the circles.
4 To make the birds, use the card template and work on the white side of each sheet of metallic card. Place the bird shape in every possible space, turning it to left and right to form 'pairs'. Mark with a pencil and cut out the birds using the sharp pointed scissors. Mix and match the coloured birds, so that one side is green and the other blue.
5 With the white side of the birds uppermost, and matching the pairs, apply a thin coat of adhesive, and leave it to become tacky. Join each bird shape. Leave birds to dry completely.
6 Using one side of the hole puncher, make a hole on the back of each bird as shown on the pattern. If some bird pairs do not match evenly, then trim away any white or jagged edges which look unattractive.
7 Cut the length of ribbon into twelve 50 cm (20 in) lengths.
8 Use two 50 cm (20 in) lengths of ribbon to hang the mobile. Tie each end securely in holes on opposite sides of the card circle.

Thread and knot three or four birds to each of the remaining ten ribbon lengths. Thread these ribbon lengths into holes on the card circle, using two

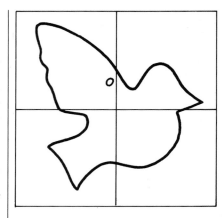

Scale 1 square = 5 cm (approx 2 in)

holes for each length, and knot each one securely. To correct the balance of the mobile and keep the card circle horizontal, remove or add birds.

RAINBOW SLIPPERS

The pastel rainbow shades of these slippers are as soft as the wool from which they are made. A large, loosely tied knot of yarn decorates the toe.

materials to make 2 slippers

50 g (2 oz) ball mohair
1 pair of 4½ mm needles (size 8)

to make

Work throughout in stocking stitch. Cast on 32 stitches. Work 4 rows.

Increase 1 stitch at each end of the next row and every following fourth row until you have 40 stitches.

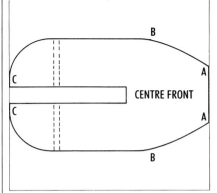

Work 13 rows straight.

Next row: knit 18. Leave these stitches on a stitchholder. Cast off next 4 stitches. Knit to end.

Continue on these 18 stitches. Work 39 rows straight. Decrease 1 stitch at outer edge only on next 4 knit rows. Cast off remaining 14 stitches.

Rejoin yarn to inner edge of remaining stitches and complete to match first side. You should end up with a shape resembling the diagram shown here. Make the second slipper in the same way.

Refer to yarn label for pressing instructions.

To make up slippers, fold knitted piece lengthways with right sides together. Match A to A, B to B and C to C. Oversew from centre front to C to form a flat seam. To decorate the slippers, divide the remaining length of yarn into two. Keeping strands in one straight bundle, form two loose bows. Catchstitch the bows to the slippers.

ADULTS' BIRTHDAYS

The fun need not go out of giving at birthdays
for older members of the family. Bring some
humour into the present , as well as making sure that
they are useful.
Personalize a director's chair with the letters DAD.
These are cut out from dark brown hessian fused on
bondaweb and then attached to the back of the chair.
As an extra you could also stitch together a hessian
drawstring bag or a cream canvas pouch.
An old deckchair can easily be renovated and given
an individual designer look with a fresh coat of paint,
and a bright red balloon motif stitched on to the
canvas. There are also instructions for making a red
canvas bag to go with the deckchair – handy for
holding suntan cream, sunglasses and a paperback.
The most impressive present in this chapter is a fish
bedcover made from crisp white sheeting and blue
and green nylon netting. Three large fishes are
highlighted with blue and green net trimmings.
For the sports enthusiast, make a simple shoe bag
from black and white ticking and lined with red PVC
to hold trainers. It has the owner's initials stitched on
the front, so that it can't easily be mislaid in the
changing rooms. There are two designs to choose
from: a drawstring bag or a bag with a flap.

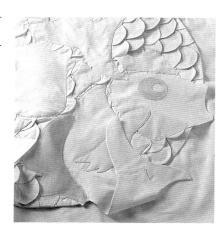

Right Summer evenings on the patio
with a cool drink, canapés and some
surprise presents. The deckchair has been
decorated with a red balloon and given a
coat of paint – the red-and-white
gingham bows belong to a canvas bag
which is specially designed to hang on the
back of the deckchair. On the right, the
director's chair is personalized with the
letters DAD, and a hessian bag matching
hangs off the arm rest. The ticking shoe
bag on the deckchair is an excellent
present for anyone keen on sport.
Left One of the three fishes which make
up the fish bedcover.

TICKING SHOE BAGS

Despite their snazzy appearance, these shoe bags are extremely practical and hard-wearing. They are both made from strong striped mattress ticking lined with waterproof kiss-laminated PVC. One of the ticking bags is bound with cotton bias binding and has a flap fastened with decorative matching pom-pons. The other has a drawstring to close the top and is decorated with a big PVC initial to identify the name of the owner.

BAG WITH FLAP

material

- 31 cm (12 in) of 145 cm (57 in)-wide mattress ticking
- 31 cm (12 in) of 129 cm (51 in)-wide kiss-laminated PVC
- 1.5 m (59 in) of 2.5 cm (1 in)-wide smoke-grey cotton bias binding
- 2 × 5 cm (2 in)-diameter wool pom-pons, 1 red, 1 white
- matching thread (grey)
- centimetre pattern paper
- ruler, scissors, pencil, ballpoint pen

to make

1 Transfer the diagram to centimetre pattern paper. Using this as your pattern, cut the following:
from mattress ticking (using pencil) 1 bag shape
from PVC (using ballpoint pen on the wrong side of a single thickness) 1 bag shape
from bias binding 1 × 32 cm (12½ in) length, 1 × 114 cm (44¾ in) length.

2 Attach the lining to the bag. Place the wrong side of the PVC to the wrong side of the ticking, matching the raw edges and flat ends. Pin and tack round all four sides.

3 Wrap the wrong side of the shorter length of binding over the raw edge of the short edge of the bag shape. Neaten the ends by turning 1 cm (⅜ in) to the wrong side. Pin and tack to hold. Machine stitch as close to the inner edge of binding as possible.

4 To make a bag shape, bring the bound end of the bag up to meet the base of the flap (as shown on the diagram). Pin and tack with 6 mm (¼ in) turnings down the sides of the bag to hold.

5 Bind the sides and flap of the bag using the longer length of bias binding. Neaten the end, beginning at the bottom left-hand edge. Wrap the binding evenly round the raw edges of the tacked PVC and ticking. Pin, tack and machine stitch, working up the left side, around the flap and down the right side. Remove any visible tacking.

6 Position one pom-pon on the flap and the other centrally on the front of the bag approximately 15 cm (6 in) from bound top edge. Catchstitch them to the bag. Tie long ends of wool from the top pom-pon around the other to keep the bag securely closed.

POM-PON

materials

- 2 × 7.5 cm (3 in) squares of card
- pencil, scissors, compasses
- double knitting wool

to make

1 Draw a circle 7.5 cm (3 in) in diameter on each of the pieces of card and cut them out. Draw two second circles 3 cm (1¼ in) in diameter exactly in the

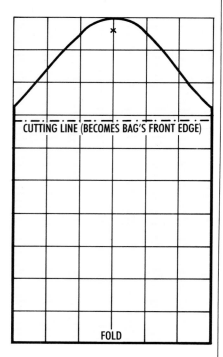

Scale 1 square = 5 cm (approx 2 in)

CUTTING LINE (BECOMES BAG'S FRONT EDGE)

FOLD

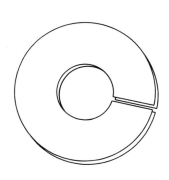

1 To make a pom-pon, cut out two rings from card, with a diameter of 7 cm (2¼ in) and a hole measuring 3 cm (1¼ in). Place the rings together. Cut a slit for wool to pass through.

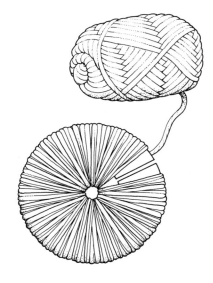

2 Wind the wool firmly around the cardboard rings. Working evenly, cover all the card and continue until the hole in the centre is completely filled.

middle of each circle of card and cut them out to give a ring shape. Place the two cards together.

2 Make an opening for wool to pass through easily by cutting a slit through both card circles.

3 Bind the wool firmly round the card circles with a continuous winding action. Work evenly round the circles until the centre hole is filled with the wool.

4 Slip the blade of the scissors between the card circles and cut right round the edge through all layers of wrapped wool.

5 Take two 30 cm (11¾ in) lengths of wool and place them between the two card circles so that the wool is halfway along the pom-pon. Tie a knot in the lengths of wool, and pull firmly around the strands of the pom-pon. Pull the card circles apart and fluff up the strands of yarn.

6 If necessary, trim the pom-pon to give a smooth ball shape.

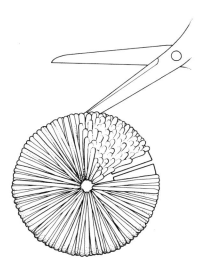

3 Slip one blade of a sharp pair of scissors between the two card rings and cut carefully around the edge through all the layers of the bound wool.

4 Place two 30 cm (11¾ in) lengths of wool between the two card rings, pull and tie in a knot. Remove the card rings from the pom-pon and fluff up the wool. Trim to neaten.

DRAWSTRING BAG

materials

30 cm (11¾ in) of 145 cm (57 in)-wide mattress ticking

30 cm (11¾ in) of 150 cm (59 in)-wide red cotton-backed PVC

1 m (39½ in) each of cord in black, red and white

matching thread (red, white)

centimetre pattern paper

medium safety pin

scissors, pencil, ruler, teflon foot

to make

1 Transfer the diagrams to centimetre pattern paper. Using these as your patterns, cut the following:

from mattress ticking 1 bag shape

from PVC 1 extended bag shape, 1 initial shape.

2 To make the lining, fold the PVC oblong in half lengthways with right sides together. With 6 mm (¼ in) turnings, pin, tack and machine stitch down the side seams. Leave an opening between the notches for the cord. Remove tacking. Flatten the turnings on the notched opening to the wrong side and topstitch around the opening to secure. Make sure you keep the lining bag to the wrong side.

3 Position the top of the PVC intitial on the right side of the ticking bag shape, approximately 13 cm (5 in) from the top edge. Pin, tack and machine stitch 3 mm (⅛ in) from the edges of the initial.

4 To make the ticking bag, fold the ticking oblong in half with right sides together and matching raw edges. Pin, tack and machine stitch the side seams with 6 mm (¼ in) turnings. Remove tacking.

5 Insert the PVC lining bag into the ticking bag. With the wrong side of the PVC to the wrong side of the ticking, slide the longer PVC bag into the ticking bag. Bring the top edge of the PVC out and over on to the right side of the ticking to a depth of approximately 5.5 cm (2¼ in). Pin and tack in position. Topstitch the top edge with three lines of machine stitching, at 3 mm (⅛ in), 2.5 cm (1 in) and 5 cm (2 in) intervals from the top edge of the bag. Remove the tacking.

6 Knot one end of each length of cord together and braid them. Knot the other end. Attach the safety pin to one end of the cord. Slide the pin into the casing through the opening and feed it along. Bring it out again at the same opening. Remove the safety pin. Pull up the cord and knot it to close the top of the bag. It is now finished.

USING PVC

PVC is a woven or knitted cotton backing, coated with polyvinyl chloride. A durable fabric, it is suitable for making items which need to be waterproof. It is simple to work with as the cotton side is easily marked and, once cut, will not fray.

Scale 1 square = 5 cm (approx 2 in)

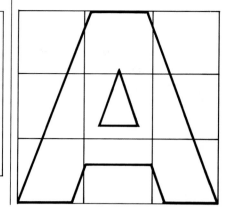

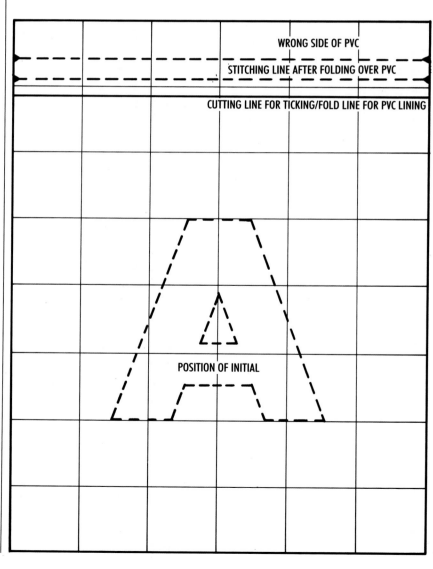

WRONG SIDE OF PVC

STITCHING LINE AFTER FOLDING OVER PVC

CUTTING LINE FOR TICKING/FOLD LINE FOR PVC LINING

POSITION OF INITIAL

FISH BEDCOVER

Three different fishes splash on a fish scale background to add a whimsical touch to a plain bedcover. The scaly background and the fins are outlined and accented with nylon net – we have used sea-green and ocean-blue. You could use other colours to co-ordinate with your bedroom decor.

The fish and their background are assembled and appliquéd to a circle of plain sheeting.

materials

2 m (2¼ yd) of 228 cm (90 in)-wide white polyester cotton sheeting
1 m (39½ in) of 1 m (39½ in)-wide emerald green nylon net
50 cm (20 in) of 1 m (39½ in)-wide blue nylon net
3 m (3¼ yd) of 82 cm (32¼ in)-wide iron-on medium-weight vilene
matching thread (white)
centimetre pattern paper
scissors, pencil, ballpoint pen

Scale   1 square = 5 cm (approx 2 in)

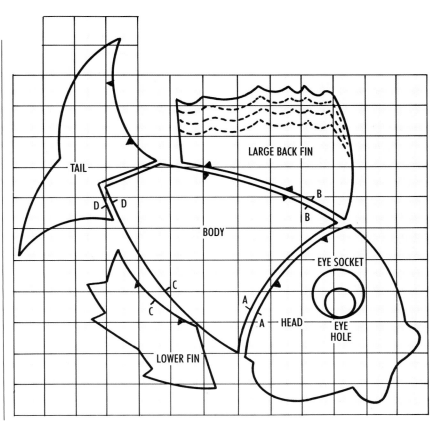

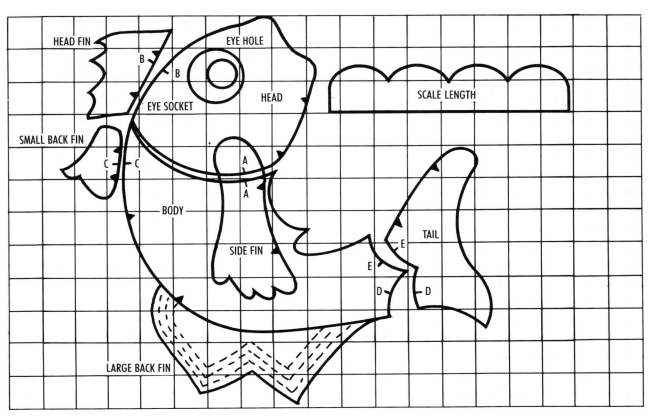

to make

1 Transfer the diagrams to centimetre pattern paper. Using these as your patterns, cut the following:

from sheeting each section of each fish twice, 2 × 87cm (34 in) circles, 50 scale lengths, 3 eye socket circles

from green net 25 scale lengths, 3 eye socket circles

from blue net 3 sets of four large back fins, each cut smaller than the last (as indicated on pattern)

from vilene each section of each fish once.

2 Fuse each vilene fish section to the wrong side of one corresponding sheeting fish section on all three fishes.

3 On all fishes, join each fish section by matching each sheeting 'pair' with vilene side to one unfused side. Pin, tack and machine stitch with 6mm (¼ in) turnings, beginning and ending at notched openings. Remove tacking.

4 Turn fish sections through to right side. Roll out seams to edge, sliding turnings on opening to inside but keeping any curve or shape of fish section. Pin, tack and press round edges.

5 Join green net eyes to fused sheeting eyes and then to head sections, catch-stitching with tiny stitches.

6 Match the 50 scale lengths to form 25 pairs. Pin, tack and machine stitch with 6mm (¼ in) turnings. Snip into curves. Remove tacking. Turn to right side. Press. Place corresponding single green net scale lengths to back of turned scales. Pin and tack across straight edge.

7 Arrange sections of each fish as in photograph and diagram, on one large sheeting circle. Fill the empty spaces between fishes with the rows of scales, overlapping the straight edge of the scales with the shaped edge and alternating the curved edges to form 'fish scaling'. Overlap the edge of the sheeting circle with sets of scales as necessary and trim any overlap to match edge of circle. Pin, tack and topstitch straight edges of scales and each fish section except where indicated on pattern. Some fins stand free. Keep topstitching to extreme edge on all sections. Remove all visible tacking.

8 Arrange the largest blue net back fin on the corresponding fish. Using tiny white stitches, catchstitch to sheeting fin

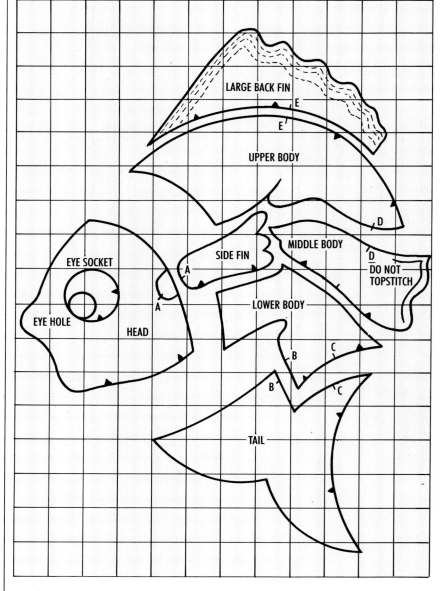

Scale 1 square = 5cm (approx 2 in)

along long curved edge. Add each back fin with the smallest on top. Repeat for each fish.

9 Fold and pin the tails of the lower and middle fish on their bodies to avoid machine line. Match second sheeting circle to right side of completed fish-covered circle, matching notched opening.

Pin, tack and machine stitch round circle with 1cm (⅜ in) turnings. Remove tacking. Turn through to right side, pushing turnings on notched opening to the inside. Catchstitch opening to close. Remove pins from tails of

fish. Roll out edges of circles. Press edge only. Curl tail of lower fish on to centre of body and catchstitch to hold.

Place the fish circle on a plain bedcover to brighten up any bedroom. Either catchstitch it to hold in position, or just lay it loose on top.

DIRECTOR'S CHAIR AND BAGS

Re-cover an old director's chair for Dad's birthday and make a matching pouch with a strong canvas strap to hold his newspapers and magazines neatly. The hessian drawstring bag is useful for carrying bits and pieces or for 'wrapping' birthday goodies. Personalize the chair by decorating it with the letters 'DAD' and monogram the drawstring bag in contrasting hessian fabric.

CHAIR

materials

25 cm (10 in) of 150 cm (59 in)-wide dark brown brough (linen union) or soft hessian
bondaweb
2 × 20 cm (8 in) squares of thin card
75 cm (29½ in) of 150 cm (59 in)-wide beige brough (linen union) or soft hessian
director's chair frame
matching thread (beige, dark brown)
centimetre pattern paper
pencil, scissors, tailor's chalk

to make

1 Cut three 20 cm (8 in) squares from dark brown brough and fuse to corresponding squares of bondaweb.

2 Transfer the 'D' and 'A' letters to centimetre pattern paper and then to thin card. Using these as your patterns, cut the following:
from brown brough backed with bondaweb 'D A D' letters
from beige brough 1 chair back strip 120 cm (47 in) × 23.5 cm (9¼ in), 1 seat oblong 1 m (39½ in) × 46 cm (18 in).

3 Remove the paper backing from each fused letter. Position the letter 'A' in the centre of the chair strip. With a space of 2 cm (¾ in), position the two 'D's on either side. Using a warm, dry iron, fuse the letters to the back strip. The word 'D A D' will be on the back of the director's chair and the short seam will be at the front.

4 Join the short ends on the beige back strip with 1 cm (⅜ in) turnings. Pin, tack and machine stitch to form a circle. Press seam open. Remove tacking. Turn a 1 cm (⅜ in) hem to wrong side on both long edges. Pin, tack and machine stitch. Press. Turn to right side. Flatten circular shape, placing the short seam at centre front. Pin, tack and topstitch 6 mm (¼ in) across top edge of chair back, through both thicknesses. Form two vertical casing lines from top to bottom of chair back, by measuring 6 cm (2⅜ in) in from both folded sides. Pin, tack and machine stitch on these lines to form the tubular casing for the wooden uprights. Join lower edges of back strip by topstitching through both layers **between** the tubular casings. The seam will be approximately 47 cm (18½ in) long. Remove tacking.

5 With right sides together, join the short ends of the seat oblong with 1 cm (⅜ in) turnings. Pin, tack and machine stitch. Press seam open. Turn a 1 cm (⅜ in) hem to wrong side on both long edges of the tube shape. Pin, tack and machine stitch. Press. Turn tube to right side. Place the seam at the centre back and flatten the tube shape. Pin to hold. Form the side rod casings by marking a line with pins on each side, parallel to and 2 cm (¾ in) in from the folded sides. Mark a line with tacking and topstitch through both thicknesses from front seat edge to back seat edge. Remove visible tacking.

6 Slide rods into side hems of seat. Push the covered rods into the carved channels. Slide personalized chair back on to wooden uprights.

DRAWSTRING BAG

materials

20 cm (8 in) square of cream brough (linen
    union) or hessian
bondaweb
20 cm (8 in) square of thin card
30 cm (11¾ in) of 150 cm (59 in)-wide coffee
    brough (linen union) or hessian
85 cm (33½ in) length of white cord
matching thread (cream, brown)
centimetre pattern paper
safety pin, scissors, pencil, iron

to make

1 Fuse the 20cm (8in) square of
cream hessian to a 20cm (8in) square
of bondaweb.

2 Transfer the letter 'D' to the centimetre pattern paper and then to the
thin card. Mark the letter on the backing
paper of the fused cream hessian
square. From the coffee hessian, cut
two 42 × 30cm (16½ × 11¾in)
oblongs.

3 Cut out the letter 'D' from the cream
hessian square. Remove paper backing
and using a warm dry iron, fuse the
letter to one coffee hessian oblong,
placing the base of letter 'D' parallel to
and 6cm (2⅜in) from one short end.
Topstitch round the letter on the extreme edge.

4 With 'D' side to right side of second
oblong, join oblongs. Pin, tack and
machine stitch with 1cm (⅜in) turnings, across one short end and down
one long side. On remaining long side,
pin, tack and machine stitch 7cm
(2¾in) from open short end. Leave a
1cm (⅜in) gap, then continue machine
line to bottom of bag. Press seam and
turning on gap open.

5 Turn a 6mm (¼in) hem to wrong
side along top open end of bag. Pin and
tack. Turn in a further 4cm (1½in)
hem. Pin, tack and machine stitch.

6 Topstitch two lines around top of
bag 2cm (¾in) and 4cm (1½in) from
folded top edge on either side of the
1cm (⅜in) opening to form the casing
for the cord.

7 Using the safety pin, thread the white
cord through the opening on the side
seam and along the topstitched casing.
Knot ends together and pull up!

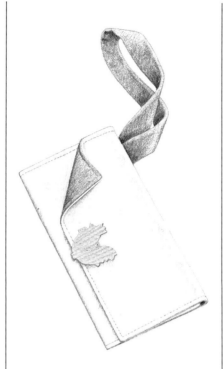

Scale 1 square = 5 cm (approx 2 in)

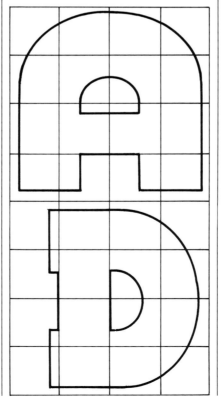

CANVAS POUCH

materials

40 cm (15¾ in) of 44 cm (17¼ in)-wide coffee
    deckchair canvas
30 cm (11¾ in) of 44 cm (17¼ in)-wide cream
    deckchair canvas
matching thread (brown, cream)
wooden toggle or large wooden button
tailor's chalk, pencil, scissors, iron

to make

1 Cut the following:
from coffee canvas 44cm (17¼in) × 29cm
(11½in) oblong (lining), 24cm (9½in)
× 8cm (3in) oblong (strap)
from cream canvas 44cm (17¼in) × 29cm
(11½in) oblong (bag).

2 Mark canvas bag oblong by notching
a 15cm (6in) opening centrally on one
long side.

3 With right sides together, beginning
and ending at the notched opening, join
the cream and coffee oblongs with 1cm
(⅜in) turnings. Trim corners. Turn
through to right side. Roll out edges
and tuck turnings on the opening to the
inside. Pin and tack.

4 Form the pocket of the bag by
folding one short end of pouch shape
(coffee sides together) 13cm (5in) on
to bag oblong. Pin and tack. Topstitch
along outside edges on extreme edge
round complete pouch oblongs, catching in the sides of the pocket. Remove
tacking.

5 With right sides together and taking
6mm (¼in) turnings, pin, tack and
machine stitch strap oblong across one
short end and down long edge. Trim
corners. Using a ruler, push stitched
short end through to right side. Turn in
6mm (¼in) on the open short end.
Press. Match the turned short ends
together and place them on the outside
of the cream canvas pouch, approximately 14cm (5½in) from flap edge.
Pin, tack and topstitch each short end of
strap to pouch, forming the strap into a
loop shape. Remove tacking.

6 Sew decorative toggle or button to
centre front of flap.

DECKCHAIR AND BAG

A fly-away balloon has landed on this smart deckchair. The seat is made of strong canvas and the frame has been painted matt black. Tied to the back of the chair is a practical canvas bag. It holds all your supplies for a day at the beach or a lazy afternoon in the garden and converts quickly to a handy shoulder bag by re-tying the gingham straps.

DECKCHAIR

materials

deckchair frame
sandpaper, 2.5 cm (1 in) paintbrush
1 small tin undercoat
1 small tin matt black paint
1.5 m (59 in) of 44 cm (17¼ in)-wide oatmeal deckchair canvas
30 cm (11¾ in) square of red canvas
30 cm (11¾ in) square of red polyester/cotton
90 cm (36 in)-long black bootlace or black cord
matching thread (oatmeal, red, black)
centimetre pattern paper
scissors, pencil

to make

1   Sand the deckchair frame and apply one coat of undercoat. When dry, apply one coat of matt black paint. When dry, apply a second coat of black paint and let it dry completely before attaching the canvas seat.
2   Transfer the diagram to centimetre pattern paper. Using this as your pattern, cut the following:
from oatmeal canvas 1 piece 1.5 m (59 in) long of the correct width for the chair
from red canvas 1 balloon shape
from red polyester/cotton 1 balloon shape.
3   Match the canvas and the polyester/cotton balloon shapes with right sides together. With 6 mm (¼ in) turnings, pin, tack and machine stitch leaving a 7 cm (2¾ in) opening. Snip curves. Remove tacking. Turn to right side. Roll the seam to the edge, pushing out the neck of the balloon and turning the seam allowance on the opening to the inside. Pin and tack the opening. Press lightly.

4   Position the top of the balloon approximately 25 cm (10 in) from the top short side of the oatmeal canvas, leaning the balloon to the right as in the photograph. Pin and tack in place. Slide one end of the bootlace under the neck of the balloon, leaving 15 cm (6 in) free to tie up later. Topstitch round the balloon 2 mm (¹⁄₁₆ in) from the edge, catching in the bootlace behind the neck of the balloon. Tie the bootlace around the neck. Swirl the long end of the bootlace down and across the canvas. Pin, tack and topstitch in place.
5   Turn a 5 cm (2 in) hem on each short end of the oatmeal canvas. Slide the crossbar rods from the deckchair into the turned hems, and position the covered rods in the openings on the deckchair frame.

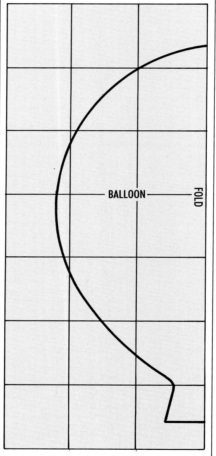

Scale   1 square = 5 cm (approx 2 in)

BAG

materials

1 m (39½ in) of 44 cm (17¼ in)-wide red deckchair canvas
1 m (39½ in) of 115 cm (45 in)-wide red-and-white gingham
1 m (39½ in) of 82 cm (32¼ in)-wide craft-quality vilene
45 cm (17¾ in) of 1 m (39½ in)-wide white plastic lining
2.1 m (83 in) length of 2.5 cm (1 in)-wide red cotton bias binding
20 cm (8 in) of 82 cm (32¼ in)-wide iron-on vilene
3 × 2 cm (¾ in)-diameter white plastic curtain rings
matching thread (red)
centimetre pattern paper
tailor's chalk, scissors, pencil, teflon foot

to make

1   Transfer the diagrams to centimetre pattern paper, and cut out the following:
from deckchair canvas cut one 92 cm (36½ in) × 44 cm (17¼ in) oblong, place pattern on each end and trim corners.
from gingham cut one 37 cm (14½ in) × 44 cm (17¼ in) oblong, place pattern on one end and trim corners, cut 4 straps.
from craft-quality vilene cut one 92 cm (36½ in) × 44 cm (17¼ in) oblong, place pattern on each end and trim corners.
from plastic lining cut one 57 cm (22½ in) × 44 cm (17¼ in) oblong, place pattern on one end and trim corners.

FOLD   STRAP

from bias binding 1 × 44cm (17¼in) length, 1 × 160cm (63in) length
from iron-on vilene 2 straps.

2 Place the 44cm (17¼in) straight edges of the plastic lining and gingham oblongs together with right sides facing, matching raw edges. With 1cm (⅜in) turnings, pin, tack, and machine stitch, using the teflon foot. Remove tacking. Laid flat, this piece forms the bag lining.

3 Sandwich the craft vilene between the wrong sides of the gingham/plastic lining and the canvas oblong. Pin and tack 6mm (¼in) round all edges.

4 Open out the 44cm (17¼in) length of bias binding. With right sides together and matching the raw edge to the 44cm (17¼in) straight edge of the bag, pin, tack and machine stitch along the 1.2cm (½in) bias crease. Remove tacking. Turn the binding to the plastic part of the lining. Pin, tack and catch-stitch the fold to the plastic. Remove tacking.

5 Fold the bag oblong lengthways, placing the bias-bound short edge to the notches on the flap. Matching raw edges and with 6mm (¼in) turnings, pin and tack the side edges to hold.

6 Open out the 160cm (63in) length of bias binding and place one end to the bottom left corner of the front of the bag (the flap side), with right sides together. Matching raw edges and turning 1cm (⅜in) on the short end to the inside of the binding to give a neat finish, pin, tack and machine stitch the binding to the bag. Work up the left side, round the flap and down the right side, neatening with 1cm (⅜in) to the inside at the bottom edges. Fold binding to the other side and catchstitch the entire length. Remove any visible tacking.

7 Make the straps. Fuse the iron-on vilene to the wrong side of two gingham straps. With right sides of gingham together, place one reinforced strap to one plain one, matching the raw edges. With 6mm (¼in) turnings, pin, tack and machine stitch from notch to notch round the straps, leaving the 15cm (6in) opening. Snip curves. Remove tacking. Turn the straps to the right side and roll the seams to the edge. Pin, tack and press lightly. Turn the seam allowance to the inside at the opening and catchstitch. Remove tacking. Press lightly. Topstitch 6mm (¼in) from the edges.

8 Oversew the white plastic curtain rings to the back of the bag. Position them evenly just below the fold of the flap, one at each top corner and one in the centre.

9 To hang the bag from the deckchair, slide each strap through one outer ring, and tie each one to the top bar of the deckchair frame. To use as a shoulder bag, slide one end of one strap through one outer ring. Slide one end of the second strap through the other two rings to meet it. Tie the ends of the straps in a double knot. Double-knot the other ends to make a loop handle.

WEDDINGS AND CHRISTENINGS

A wedding is an occasion when virtually everything becomes a memento. For the marriage service, make fabric posies to attach to the pew ends, using bridal taffeta, cream satin ribbons and pearl beads.

At the reception which follows, it would be a monumental undertaking to do the tablecloths for every table. But you could draw attention to the one holding the wedding cake by decorating the cloth with lamé leaves and a glittering garland. The tablecloth in this chapter is made in jade green, but obviously you could vary the colour to tie in with the colour scheme of the bride's bouquet: pale pink, lemon yellow, blue or a delicate apricot. Alternatively have a white table cloth with just gold or silver lamé decorations.

Christenings present a great opportunity for the needlewoman to reach for her sewing machine. If the family hasn't a robe which has been handed down, here is the chance to make a stunning heirloom for future generations to admire.

If making an entire set of Christening garments seems too demanding, try your hand at some simpler gifts: a cot cover quilted in pretty pale green fabric and a contrasting floral print, then decorated with a butterfly motif. There is also a pattern for a small pillow case. Or make some felt birds to string along the cot.

in this chapter

- Celebration tablecloth
- Church posy
- Christening set
- Butterfly cot cover
- Cot toy with bells

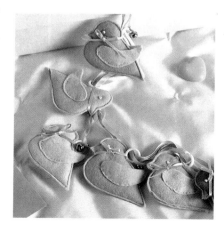

Right A display of some of the gifts you could make to mark a wedding or Christening. Draped over the stair bannisters is the corner of the butterfly cot cover and a cot toy made from felt birds and gold bells. The Christening robe hangs to the left of the cot cover and you can see the jade green celebration tablecloth above it. Look on the hall table for the church posy, ready to be taken to the church and carefully arranged on the end of a pew.

Left A detail of the cot toy with bells, for stringing across a cot or pram to keep the baby amused.

CELEBRATION TABLECLOTH

Whether you are celebrating a wedding, christening or birthday, finding a special place for the cake can present a problem. Transform a typical garden table with this splendid cloth and garland made in the bride's chosen colour and create the ideal focal point for the great event.

materials

3 m (3¼ yd) of 228 cm (90 in)-wide turquoise polyester/cotton sheeting
bondaweb
2 m (80 in) of 115 cm (45 in)-wide turquoise lamé
2 m (80 in) of 115 cm (45 in)-wide turquoise lamé overprinted with white
1 m (39½ in) of 115 cm (45 in)-wide silver lamé
5 m (5½ yd) of no. 6 cotton piping cord boiled and dried to avoid shrinkage
matching thread (turquoise)
12 bundles confectioner's silver leaves
50 silver baubles
centimetre pattern paper
16 cm (6¼ in) square of card
pencil, tailor's chalk, ballpoint pen, iron

Scale 1 square = 5 cm (approx 2 in)

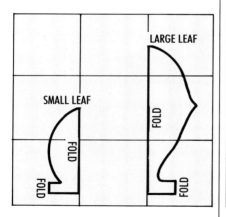

NOTE This cloth is for a table 60 cm (23½ in) in diameter and 75 cm (29½ in) high. To alter the pattern to fit your table, measure across the top of your table and add twice the drop (measurement from your table top to the floor). Then add 3.5 cm (1⅜ in) for the hem.

to make

1 Copy the diagram for a quarter circle and alter accordingly after checking measurements of your table. Transfer the leaf designs to centimetre pattern paper and then to the piece of card for easier marking. Using these as your patterns, cut a square from sheeting fabric measuring 2.25 m (88½ in). Fold the square in half and then in half again. Cut a circle, using the quarter circle pattern.

2 Turn a 6 mm (¼ in) hem to wrong side. Then turn a further 1 cm (⅜ in) hem. Pin, tack and machine stitch.

3 Using a warm dry iron, fuse the bondaweb to the wrong side of the three lamé fabrics and the remaining

A LARGE, CIRCULAR CLOTH

Working with such a large item demands plenty of space, so make sure your sewing machine is on a good-sized table, cleared of all the needles and boxes of pins. When turning a fine hem on a circular cloth, try to keep the hem as narrow as possible. It will start to pleat, and the turned edge to poke, if it is too deep.

polyester. Keep the paper backing intact for marking. Using the card patterns and ballpoint pen, mark a continuous chain of leaves, turning along selvedge and length of bondaweb paper. Cut out the leaf shapes in a chain, keeping back 20 of each colour lamé single-coated small leaf for the tablecloth.

4 Peel off paper and position the chain of leaves on the straight grain and wrong side of the remaining lamé material. Fuse both pieces of lamé with a warm dry iron. Cut out the chain. (You may have to catch the light once the lamés are fused in order to see outline of first lamé leaf.)

5 Fold each lamé leaf lengthways and form a 'spine' with a line of machine stitching.

6 Wind the lamé leaves round the full length of piping cord, alternating silver, turquoise, printed and polyester/cotton leaves. Decorate with confectioner's leaves and silver baubles. Trim the remaining 20 lamé leaves of each colour from the chain, fuse and scatter on cloth. Cover the table with cloth and arrange the garland as in the photograph, pinning and catchstitching to secure it to the cloth.

Scale 1 square = 10 cm (approx 4 in)

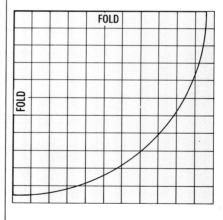

CHURCH POSY

Made from scraps of wedding gown or bridesmaid's dress fabric, this posy echoes the bride's traditional bouquet and after the event will provide a lasting reminder of the happy day. Flower circles and lily and petal shapes are decorated with pearls and tied together with satin ribbons. Loops of ribbon attached to the back of the stiffened background circles of bridal taffeta make it suitable for decorating a special family pew.

materials to make 1 posy

40 cm (15¾ in) of 115 cm (45 in)-wide bridal taffeta
bondaweb
20 cm (8 in) of 82 cm (32¼ in)-wide craft-quality vilene
60 seed pearls
1.5 cm (⅝ in)-diameter pearl
3 × 38 cm (15 in) of 3 mm (⅛ in)-wide cream or white ribbon
4 × 31 cm (12 in) long white 6 mm (¼ in) chenille pipecleaners
fabric adhesive, scissors, pencil
7 × 5 mm (³⁄₁₆ in)-diameter pearls (for flower centres)
5 m (5½ yd) of 6 mm (¼ in)-wide cream double satin ribbon
matching thread (cream)
centimetre pattern paper
10 cm (4 in) square of card for leaf

to make

1 Cut squares or oblongs of bridal taffeta big enough to hold the flower head shapes, and fuse the fabric to bondaweb, pressing with a warm dry iron.
2 Transfer the diagrams to centimetre pattern paper. Using these as your patterns, cut the following:
from bridal taffeta 2 backing circles, 1.25 m (49 in) of 5 cm (2 in)-wide bias strip
from bondaweb-backed oblongs of bridal taffeta 2 four-petalled flowers, 6 flower heads, 4 large lily shapes, 4 small lily shapes
from vilene 1 backing circle.
3 Fuse the vilene circle to the wrong side of one backing circle of taffeta with bondaweb. Spacing evenly and approximately 6 mm (¼ in) in from edge of circle, sew the 60 seed pearls to the

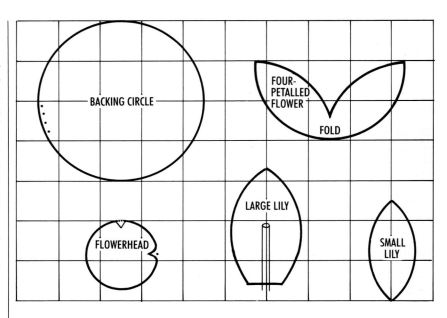

Scale 1 square = 5 cm (approx 2 in)

taffeta side of the vilene-backed circle. Fuse the second taffeta circle to the vilene-backed front circle, pressing lightly so as not to crack the beads.
4 Remove the paper backing from bondaweb and fuse the three pairs of taffeta flower heads together. Revolve the flower head pattern to create two flowers, each with four petals.
5 Fuse pair of four-petalled flowers together.
6 Fuse pairs of large and small lily shapes together.
7 Sew the 1.5 cm (⅝ in) pearl to the centre of the four-petalled flower heads.
8 Sew the 5 mm (³⁄₁₆ in) pearls to the centre of the three flower heads.
9 Cut the 1.25 m (49 in) length of bias strip into four equal parts. With right sides together, fold each bias strip in half lengthways, placing a 38 cm (15 in) length of ribbon in fold of fabric.
10 Pin, tack and machine stitch across the short end of the rouleau strip, securing the ribbon. Pin, tack and machine stitch down the long edge, approximately 6 mm (¼ in) from folded edge. Trim turnings down to 3 mm (⅛ in). Holding short stitched end in one hand, pull the protruding ribbon with the other to turn the rouleau casing to the right side. Trim away short stitched end, releasing ribbon from inside rouleau. Repeat process for each

bias strip.
11 Slide the four rouleau lengths on to the three chenille pipe cleaners.
12 Catchstitch each of the three flower heads and the four petalled flower to each end of two rouleaux. Wrap the four lily shapes round the ends of the remaining two rouleaux, 4 cm (1½ in) from the end, to create a lily flower. Apply adhesive to one side of a 5 mm (³⁄₁₆ in) pearl and drop into open centre of protruding rouleau.
13 Bend the rouleau-covered pipe cleaners in half, bringing the flowers together.
14 Loop 2 m (2¼ yd) of the 5 m (5½ yd) length of the ribbon and form a double or treble handle for the pew.
15 Catchstitch one end of the looped ribbon to the centre of the beaded taffeta circle and again halfway to the edge.
16 Fold the remaining 3 m (3¼ yd) of ribbon equally into three. Slide these folded ribbons through the attached handle loops. Arrange posy of flowers on beaded circle and tie ribbon round centre. Knot and bow, cut the folds in the ribbons to allow ends to cascade down. Spread the flowers to display them and catchstitch to the stiffened circle.

CHRISTENING SET

This beautiful traditional christening robe and its matching bonnet and bib are all made in fine ecru taffeta. The shawl is also made in taffeta, then lined with delicate wool challis to provide warmth for a tiny baby. The pretty dove motif is repeated on each garment.

Scale 1 square = 5 cm (approx 2 in)

ROBE

materials

3 m (3¼ yd) of 115 cm (45 in)-wide ecru (cream) taffeta
matching thread (cream)
bondaweb

36 tiny seed pearl beads
3 pearl buttons, 6 mm (¼ in) diameter
centimetre pattern paper
10 cm (4 in) square of card
ruler, scissors, pencil

to make

1 Transfer the diagrams to the centimetre pattern paper. Using these as your patterns, cut the following from taffeta:

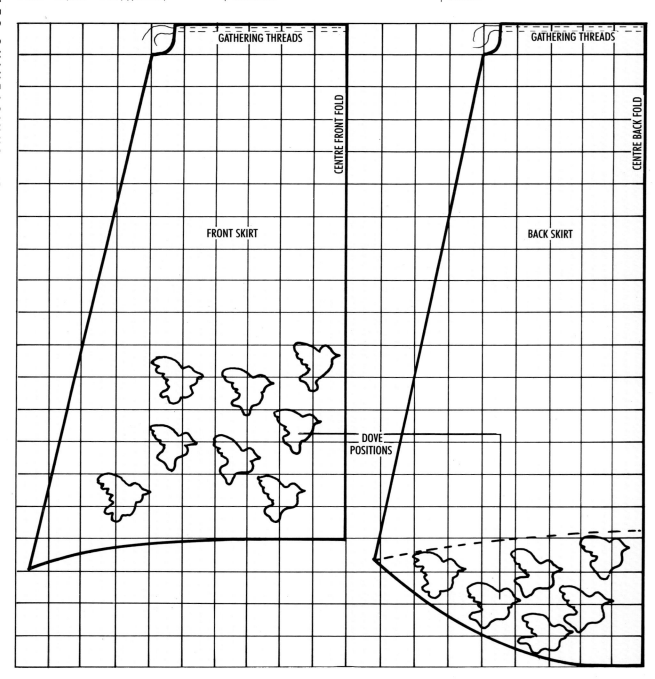

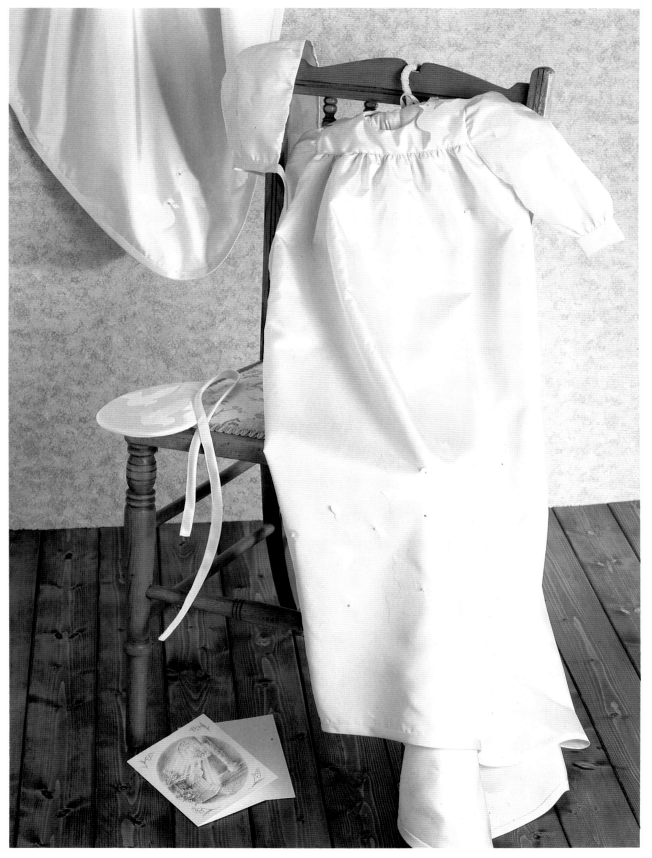

2 front skirt pieces, 2 back skirt pieces, 2 sleeve pieces, 2 cuff pieces, 2 front bodice yokes, 4 back bodice yokes, 1.75 m (69 in) of 5 cm (2 in)-wide bias strip, 40 oblongs, each 9 cm (3½ in) × 7 cm (2¾ in).

2 To make the robe, place right side of one front skirt to one back skirt. With 1 cm (⅜ in) turnings, pin, tack and machine stitch side seams. Remove tacking. Press. Join second front and back skirt pieces in same way to form the lining.

3 With right sides of the front skirts facing, match raw edges of centre back opening. Pin, tack and machine stitch round centre back opening, taking 3 mm (⅛ in) turnings. Remove tacking. Press. Turn lining skirt to inside, so that raw edges on side seams of top skirt and lining skirt are facing. Lightly press bagged-out opening.

4 Pin and tack along the doubled bodice edge of skirt. Beginning and ending at the centre back opening with large machine gathering stitch, run two lines of stitching 3 mm (⅛ in) and 6 mm (¼ in) from the raw edges.

5 With right sides of front and back bodice yoke pieces together and with 1 cm (⅜ in) turnings, pin, tack and machine stitch shoulder seams only. Remove tacking and press. Repeat for bodice lining pieces.

6 With largest machine stitch, run two lines of stitching 3 mm (⅛ in) and 6 mm (¼ in) from raw edges between notches on crown of each sleeve. Pull up to fit notches between back and front bodice yoke. With right sides together and with 1 cm (⅜ in) turnings, pin, tack and machine stitch. Remove tacking. Never press the crown on a sleeve, but push

Scale   1 square = 5 cm (approx 2 in)

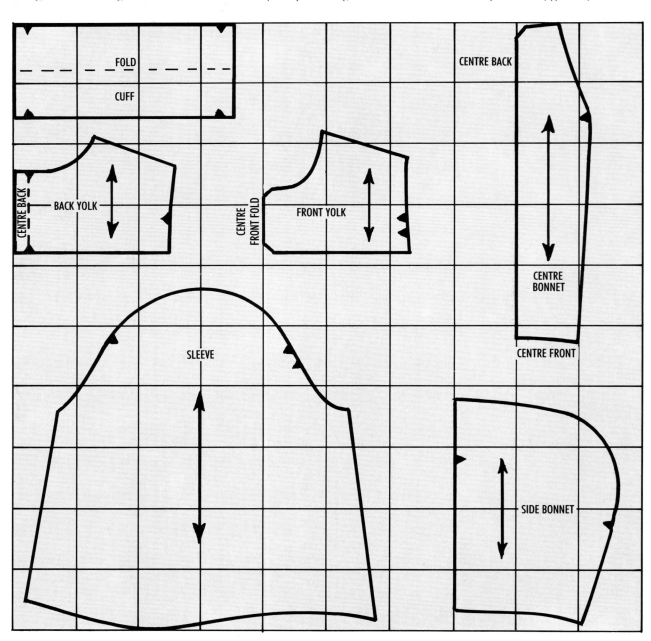

turnings down towards cuff.

7 With largest machine stitch, run two lines of stitching 3 mm (⅛ in) and 6 mm (¼ in) from raw edges of cuff edge of sleeve. Pull up to fit between notches on cuff. Pin, tack and machine stitch with 1 cm (⅜ in) turnings to join cuff to sleeve. Repeat for other sleeve.

8 With 1 cm (⅜ in) turnings, pin and tack end of cuff, sleeve seam and bodice yoke side seams. Machine stitch in one continuous line. Remove tacking. Press seam open. Repeat for other side.

9 Pull up gathered double skirts to fit bodice edge, working from centre back to centre back. Pin, tack and machine stitch to bodice yoke with 1 cm (⅜ in) turnings. Remove tacking.

10 Match right sides of bodice lining to right sides of top bodice yoke with sleeves. Taking 1 cm (⅜ in) turnings, pin, tack and machine stitch up centre back, round neckline and down centre back. Remove tacking and press. Trim turnings to 6 mm (¼ in), snip corners and into curve of neckline. Turn bodice lining through neckline open to inside. Press.

11 To neaten bodice lining, trim turning on bodice lining armhole to allow 6 mm (¼ in) to turn to inside. Pin and catchstitch to hold. Repeat for other sleeve. Turn 1 cm (⅜ in) allowance on side seams to inside, pin and catchstitch bodice side seam. Turn 1 cm (⅜ in) along base of lining bodice over gathered raw edges of skirt. Pin and catchstitch to neaten.

12 Smooth down double thickness skirt. Pin and tack 6 mm (¼ in) round hem of dress. Open out one fold of 5 cm (2 in) bias strip, matching raw edges. With right sides of bias and skirt together, pin, tack and machine stitch on first crease on binding to within 8 cm (3 in) of end of binding. Remove from machine. Match straight grains at meeting point of binding. Pin, tack and machine stitch with 6 mm (¼ in) turnings. Remove tacking and press. Continue original line of machining, matching raw edge of bias to raw edge of hem. Wrap folded half of binding over hem edges. Pin and catchstitch on second crease to inside lining of robe. Lightly press.

13 To make the doves, transfer the diagram to centimetre pattern paper and then to card and cut out. Fuse bondaweb on wrong side of the 40

9 cm (3½ in) × 7 cm (2¾ in) taffeta oblongs. Mark 20 pairs of left and right facing doves on paper backing of fused oblongs. Cut out. Peel paper from two pairs doves and fuse each to a second taffeta oblong. Cut out double thickness dove shapes with very sharp scissors. To decorate shoulders attach dove with a seed pearl 'eye', one on each shoulder seam, as in photograph approximately 1.5 cm (⅝ in) from shoulder seams. To decorate the skirt, peel off paper, arrange and fuse with a warm dry iron 36 single-thickness doves to front skirt and ten to visible shaped side of the inner back skirt, each group of 9 doves facing centre back or centre front. Catchstitch a seed pearl 'eye' to each dove. Make sure that stitches do not go through both layers of skirt.

14 Sew pearl buttons along back neck opening of the bodice. Work chain button loops to match.

BONNET

materials

50 cm (20 in) of 115 cm (45 in)-wide ecru (cream) taffeta
matching thread (cream)
bondaweb
4 tiny seed pearls beads
centimetre pattern paper
10 cm (4 in) square of card
ruler, scissors, pencil, iron

to make

1 Transfer diagrams to centimetre pattern paper. Using these as your patterns, cut the following from taffeta: 4 side bonnet pieces, 2 centre bonnet pieces, 1 m (39½ in) bias-cut taffeta strip, 5 cm (2 in) wide, 6 oblongs, each 9 cm (3½ in) × 7 cm (2¾ in).

2 With right sides together and matching raw edges and notches, join the side pieces to one centre piece. Pin, tack and machine stitch with 1 cm (⅜ in) turnings. Trim turnings to 6 mm (¼ in). Press. Repeat for bonnet lining. With right sides together, slide one completed bonnet inside other. With raw edges together and taking 1 cm (⅜ in) turnings, pin, tack and machine stitch the face edge only. Remove tacking. Trim to 6 mm (¼ in). Fold over face

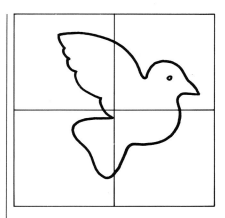

Scale 1 square = 5 cm (approx 2 in)

edge to right side. Matching raw edges, pin and tack finished face edge and raw neck edge to hold.

3 Open out one fold of the 5 cm (2 in) bias strip. With right sides together, match raw edges to double thickness at neck edge of bonnet, matching centre of bias strip to centre back notch on bonnet. Pin, tack and machine stitch on first crease on binding. Remove tacking.

Wrap folded half of binding over neck edge. Pin and tack. Topstitch 3 mm (⅛ in) along double folded edge of binding, turning 6 mm (¼ in) to inside at each short end. Remove tacking. Press lightly.

Decorate each end of tie with a double-thickness dove. Catchstitch to hold.

4 Decorate both sides of bonnet with a single-thickness dove (see step 13 of the robe).

BIB

materials

25 cm (10 in) of 115 cm (45 in)-wide ecru (cream) taffeta
16 cm (6¼ in) square of lightweight polyester wadding
matching thread (cream)
bondaweb
2 tiny seed pearl beads
centimetre pattern paper
10 cm (4 in) square of card
ruler, scissors, pencil, iron

to make

1 Transfer the diagrams to centimetre

WORKING WITH TAFFETA

When machine stitching a fine fabric like taffeta there is always the possibility that the machine's metal teeth or feed dogs might damage the underside. To prevent this, place a sheet of tissue paper under the taffeta. This will easily tear away later. If you have an old machine, loosen the pressure to prevent puckering, or tighten if the taffeta slips sideways.

pattern paper. Using these as your patterns, cut the following:

from taffeta 2 bib shapes, 75 cm (29½ in) bias-cut strip, 5 cm (2 in) wide, 2 oblongs, each 9 cm (3½ in) × 7 cm (2¾ in)

from polyester wadding 1 bib shape.

2 Match right sides of the two taffeta shapes together and the wadding shape to one wrong side. Pin, tack and machine stitch with 6 mm (¼ in) turnings. Leave neck edge open. Turn through to right side. Roll edges and tack all around to hold flat.

3 Join tie length as for bonnet. Decorate by fusing two single-thickness doves to bib front as photograph.

SHAWL

materials

1.75 m (2 yd) of 115 cm (45 in)-wide ecru polyester taffeta
1.2 m (1⅜ yd) of 150 cm (59 in)-wide cream wool challis
matching thread (cream)
bondaweb
4 tiny seed pearl beads
centimetre pattern paper
card 9 × 7 cm (3½ × 2¾ in)
scissors, pencil, iron

to make

1 Transfer the pattern for the dove and the curved corner (see page 101) to centimetre pattern paper and then to the card. Using these as your patterns, cut the following from taffeta:
trim 60 cm (23½ in) from the 1.75 m

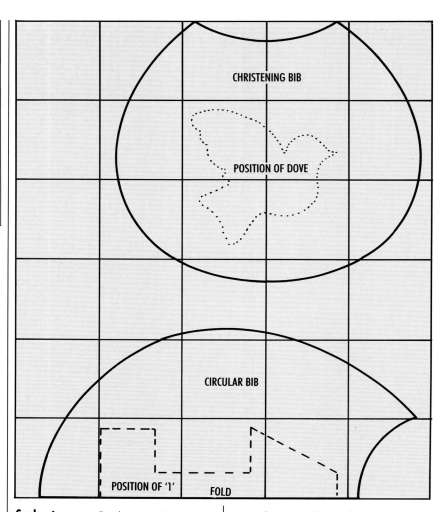

CHRISTENING BIB

POSITION OF DOVE

CIRCULAR BIB

POSITION OF 'I'   FOLD

Scale 1 square = 5 cm (approx 2 in)

(2 yd) length of taffeta to leave a perfect 115 cm (45 in) square.

Using the 60 cm (23½ in) of taffeta, make up 4.75 m (5¼ yd) of 5 cm (2 in)-wide bias binding, joined on the straight grain of fabric with 6 mm (¼ in) turnings. Press long edges to wrong side to meet at centre.

Cut 4 oblongs 9 cm (3½ in) × 7 cm (2¾ in) from remaining taffeta.

2 Matching one corner, place the wrong side of the taffeta square to the wrong side of the wool challis. Smooth both fabrics flat. Pin and tack both fabrics together, keeping stitches approximately 5 cm (2 in) from edges. Trim away excess wool challis.

3 Using the curved edge pattern, lightly mark each corner of the shawl with fine pencil dots. Trim away corners of doubled fabric on dotted line.

4 Open out one folded edge of the bias strip. With right sides together and raw edges matching, place one end of the taffeta binding to the centre of one edge of the taffeta square. Pin, tack and machine stitch the bias strip, curving binding at corners. Remove tacking.

At meeting point of binding, lightly press a 6 mm (¼ in) hem to wrong side on top binding. Continue stitching across this hem.

5 Wrap remaining folded side of binding over edges of taffeta and wool squares. Pin, tack and catchstitch the taffeta binding to the wool square. Remove any visible tacking.

6 Using a warm, dry iron, fuse bondaweb to wrong sides of taffeta oblongs.

Using the card pattern, mark two left and two right dove shapes on the paper backing of the bondaweb. Cut out. Remove paper backing. Place two facing doves on two opposite corners of the taffeta side of the shawl. Fuse with warm dry iron. Catchstitch a seed pearl 'eye' to each dove. Do not sew through both layers of the shawl.

BUTTERFLY COT COVER

Pretty pink rosebuds printed on a crisp white background provide the border of this padded pram or cot cover. The pale peppermint green centre is top-stitched for a quilted effect.

The matching pillowcase backed with plain green fabric means that the baby can sit up and enjoy an outing more.

materials

1.2 m (47 in) of 228 cm (90 in)-wide print sheeting
50 cm (20 in) of 228 cm (90 in)-wide plain green sheeting
50 cm (15¾ in) of lightweight polyester wadding
1 m (39½ in) of heavy weight polyester wadding
16 cm (6¼ in) square of white cotton lawn
40 cm (15¾ in) of 2 cm (¾ in)-wide velcro
14 cm (5½ in) of 3 mm (⅛ in)-wide dark green satin ribbon, knotted at each end
matching thread (green, white)
centimetre pattern paper
20 cm (8 in) × 30 cm (11¾ in) piece of card
yardstick, pencil, scissors, tailor's chalk

to make

1 Transfer the diagram for the butter-flies to centimetre pattern paper and then to card for easier marking. Using tailor's chalk, mark and then cut:
from print 1 oblong 97 cm (38 in) × 80 cm (31½ in)
from green 1 oblong 97 cm (38 in) × 80 cm (31½ in), 1 oblong 67 cm (26¼ in) × 50 cm (20 in)
from lightweight wadding 1 oblong 67 cm (26¼ in) × 50 cm (20 in)
from heavy weight wadding 1 oblong 97 cm (38 in) × 80 cm (31½ in).
Mark two notches 35 cm (13¾ in) apart on one long side of both print and green covers.

FOR THE BUTTERFLY

from print 1 small butterfly shape
from white lawn 1 large butterfly shape

FOR THE PILLOW

from print 1 oblong 57 cm (22½ in) × 35 cm (13¾ in)
from green 2 oblongs 57 cm (22½ in) × 22 cm (8½ in).

2 Using a yardstick, mark the topstitch-ing line on the small green oblong with a light pencil dot 10 cm (4 in) and 18 cm (7 in) from raw edges on four sides to form two oblong shapes. Match the lightweight wadding to unmarked side. Pin and tack to hold. Using green thread, topstitch along marked lines. Turn a 1 cm (⅜ in) hem on outside edges to form fabric hem. Lightly catch-stitch hem to wadding.

3 With right side of print oblong to right side of large green oblong and with 1 cm (⅜ in) turnings, pin, tack and machine stitch, leaving an opening be-tween the notches 35 cm (13¾ in) long. Press seams. Trim corners and remove tacking. Turn through to right side, pulling out corners.

4 Slide the heavy weight wadding

oblong into cover. Catchstitch opening together. Position green panel centrally on printed side of cover. Pin, tack and topstitch with green thread, 6mm (¼ in) from edge of panel to hold, machining through all layers. Remove tacking.

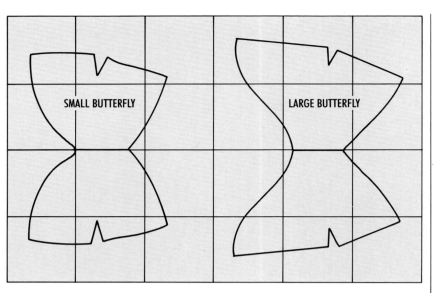

Scale 1 square = 5 cm (approx 2 in)

5 Match wrong side of print butterfly to right side of lawn shape. Pin and tack all around. Using closed zig-zag, top-stitch 6 mm (¼ in) from edge all round. Catch ribbon 'antennae' into centre top as you work. Make a pleat across the centre back of the butterfly and catch-stitch to secure. Catchstitch butterfly at centre back to bottom right hand corner of padded cover as photograph.

FOR THE PILLOW

6 On one long edge of each green oblong, turn a 1 cm (⅜ in) hem to wrong side. Pin, tack and machine stitch. Press.

7 Tear open the velcro and position the hook and loop halves centrally 1 cm (⅜ in) from the hem fold on right sides, parallel to folded edges of hem. Pin, tack and machine stitch. Remove tacking. On one oblong only, turn a further 3 cm (1¼ in), including velcro, to wrong side.

8 Press velcro pieces together, making one complete oblong. Match right sides of print oblong to assembled green back, trimming green back to match print oblong. Taking 1 cm (⅜ in) turnings, pin, tack and machine stitch all round. Remove tacking. Press seams open. Trim corners. Turn through velcro opening.

BUTTERFLY MOBILE

Make a butterfly mobile from the same fabrics as the cot cover, to hang up in the nursery. Using the butterfly patterns given for the cot cover (see page 83), cut out the shapes from the print sheeting. Next, from the plain green sheeting used for the cot cover, cut out the same number of shapes, but make them slightly smaller. Then cut more, slightly smaller shapes again, from some white cotton lawn. (Each butterfly is eventually made from three different coloured and sized pieces of material.)

Arrange the fabric shapes to make the butterflies, placing one white piece on top of one green piece on top of one printed piece. Then stitch all round the edge to hold them together. This should make an attractive border around the butterflies' wings.

Make two antennae for each butterfly, by cutting short lengths of moss green ribbon and knotting them at the ends. Stitch to the butterfly heads.

Cut longer lengths of ribbon to hang the butterflies on, allowing two or three butterflies per ribbon length.

Suspend the ribbons from a padded ring, made following the instructions for the spider mobile (see page 133), but cover it with white muslin.

COT TOY WITH BELLS

Weave a garland of pastel felt birds along the side of the cot or string it across the pram. The softly padded shapes are linked together with a delicate 'rope' of satin ribbons and decorated with bead eyes, and the tiny silver bells will keep any baby fascinated with their gentle tinkling. The birds are assembled at random to provide a delicate contrast of soft colours.

materials

22 cm (8½ in) felt square in each of the following colours: pale green, coral pink, deep peach, soft orange, deep toffee, pale toffee

20 cm (8 in) of 1 m (39½ in)-wide lightweight polyester wadding

1.75 m (2 yd) of 3 mm (⅛ in)-wide peach double satin ribbon

1.75 m (2 yd) of 3 mm (⅛ in)-wide pale blue double satin ribbon

1.5 m (1¾ yd) of 6 mm (¼ in)-wide double satin ribbon in the following colours: toffee, sugar pink, turquoise, lemon, pale blue

24 small white beads

12 × 2 cm (¾ in)-diameter plastic rings

12 × 1 cm (⅜ in)-diameter brass claw bells

centimetre pattern paper

thick card

to make

1 Transfer the diagrams to centimetre pattern paper and then to thick card. Using these as your patterns, cut the following:

from each coloured felt square 4 bird shapes, 4 wing shapes

from wadding 12 bird shapes

from peach ribbon 6 × 30 cm (11¾ in) lengths

from blue ribbon 6 × 30 cm (11¾ in) lengths.

2 Mixing colours, sandwich each polyester wadding bird shape between two felt bird shapes. Pin, tack and topstitch around extreme outside edge of birds.

3 Mix colours on wings too. Pin and tack a wing shape to each side of each padded bird. Catchstitch along lower wing, as diagram.

4 Sew a bead 'eye' to each side of the head of each bird.

5 Slip a curtain ring on to each 30 cm (11¾ in) length of 3 mm (⅛ in)-wide ribbon. Catchstitch this to a bird's neck. Tie a bow on the side of each bird's neck, and catchstitch to secure.

6 Thread one 1.5 m (1¾ yd) length of 6 mm (¼ in) ribbon through each ring. Knot a bell into the ribbon at each ring. Thread the remaining four lengths of ribbon through rings. At the ring at each end, tie the ribbons in a bundle.

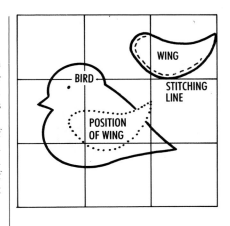

Scale 1 square = 5 cm (approx 2 in)

WEDDING ANNIVERSARIES

Giving gold, silver, ruby, pearl and crystal presents is beyond the pockets of most of us. But using glittery fabrics like lamé, and glass and pearl beads, you can stitch together some imaginative and inexpensive presents to celebrate wedding anniversaries.

A coat hanger of gold lamé decorated with gold fabric flowers makes a simple but special token on the fiftieth wedding anniversary. If you want to give more than just a coat hanger, make a scatter cushion as well, following the instructions for the silver cushion, but using gold lamé instead. For silver (25 years), two silver lamé cushions would be fitting.

Red lamé, which lends itself to the ruby anniversary (40 years), is ideal for making a pair of photo-frames. Pearl and ivory represent 30 years of marriage so make an envelope cushion from ivory taffeta and decorate it with tiny pearls.

Mark the crystal anniversary (15 years) with pure white Victoria lawn serviettes and serviette rings, decorated with glass beads, perhaps from an old necklace.

Paper, marking two years of married life, is one of the first milestones to celebrate. Fill a small basket sprayed white with shredded tissue, and little cardboard boxes containing token gifts for the occasion.

Right An imaginative assortment of gifts you could come up with for friends and relations celebrating particular wedding anniversaries: on the table, a crystal serviette set and a pair of ruby photo-frames; on the chair, a pearl and sequin envelope cushion; and arranged among tissue paper on the floor, gold and silver coat hangers and a butterfly cushion.
Left A paper dove basket full of small boxes bearing tiny gifts, and decorated with ribbons and doves.

GOLD AND SILVER GIFTS

Gold and silver lamé provide a luxurious yet inexpensive way to say congratulations on those two special anniversaries. Instructions are given here for making a gold lamé coat hanger, but you could easily make one from silver lamé for the 25th anniversary. Similarly, we have made a silver cushion here but, if you wanted, you could use gold lamé instead and change the decorations as appropriate.

GOLD COAT HANGER

materials

25 cm (10 in) of 115 cm (45 in)-wide gold lamé
25 cm (10 in) of 115 cm (45 in)-wide polyester lining
1 m (39½ in) of 1 m (39½ in)-wide lightweight polyester wadding
43 cm (17 in)-long wooden coat hanger
2 or 3 gold fabric flowers
bondaweb
matching thread (gold)
22 cm (8½ in) length of ribbon (any colour)
centimetre pattern paper
pencil, scissors

to make

1   Transfer the diagrams to the centimetre pattern paper. Using these as your patterns, cut the following:
from gold lamé 2 large hanger shapes, 2 small hanger shapes, 1 bias-cut hook casing 14 cm (5½ in) × 4 cm (1½ in), 4 squares for leaf shapes
from lining 2 large hanger shapes, 2 small hanger shapes
from wadding 2 large hanger shapes, 2 small hanger shapes, rounded ends, 6 × 1 m (39½ in) strips each 8 cm (3 in) wide, 1 hook binding strip 30 cm (11¾ in) × 3 cm (1¼ in).
2   Beginning at base of metal hook, place a long strip of wadding on the hanger and bind firmly. Working along wooden hanger, secure with tacking stitches. Continue binding towards each outer end of hanger. Repeat with remaining strips of wadding until the hanger is completely covered. Secure wadding with tacking stitches.
3   Handsew each pair of curved wadding ends together. Slide over bound

Scale   1 square = 5 cm (approx 2 in)

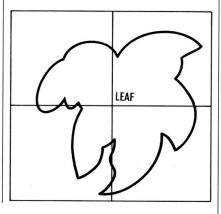

LEAF

ends of hanger and secure with tacking stitches. This will give a good shape to the finished hanger.
4   Sandwich one large wadding hanger shape between one large lining and one large lamé shape. Pin and tack. Repeat for remaining three hanger pieces.
5   Using largest machine stitch, run two gathering lines on the two large front hanger pieces as indicated on diagram, 5 mm (³⁄₁₆ in) and 6 mm (¼ in) from edge. Pull up the gathering threads until larger front hanger pieces match smaller back hanger pieces.
6   With right sides of lamé together, pin and tack both front and back hanger pieces together. Machine stitch with 1 cm (³⁄₈ in) turnings. Remove gathering threads and tacking.
7   Catchstitch one end of 30 cm (11¾ in) × 3 cm (1¼ in) strip of wadding to base of metal hook on padded hanger. Wrap firmly and secure at top of hook with tacking stitches.
8   To make the hook casing, fold the 14 cm (5½ in) × 4 cm (1½ in) strip of lamé in half lengthways, catching the 22 cm (8½ in) length of ribbon into fold. Pin, tack and machine stitch across short ends of casing, securing ribbon, and then down long sides with 1 cm (³⁄₈ in) turnings. Trim the short end, removing the protruding ribbon down to the machine line. Trim the long side down to 3 mm (¹⁄₈ in). Hold the short end firmly with one hand and pull rouleau through. Trim the ribbon away.
9   Slide casing over padded hook. Secure to wadding at base. With a knotted double length of thread in a needle, beginning at end of hook casing, run a line of fine stitches, pulling firmly for a gathered effect. Work down to the padded hanger and secure it on to the wadding.
10   Turn lamé/wadding/lining shapes halfway through to lamé sides, and slide over well-padded ends of hanger. Unfold to lamé side, taking short ends up to the covered hook. Turn 1 cm (³⁄₈ in) inside to neaten, and then catchstitch the lamé casings together at the centre line.
11   Using a warm dry iron, fuse one lamé leaf square to bondaweb. Using leaf pattern, mark leaf shape and cut out. Peel off paper and fuse leaf to a second lamé square. Cut out the leaf shape again. Repeat for the second leaf.

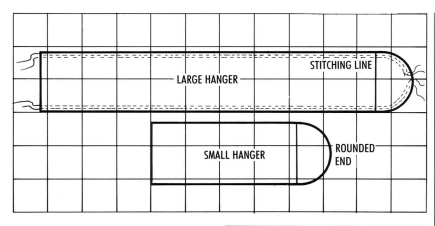

Scale 1 square = 5 cm (approx 2 in)

12 Pin a double leaf to each side of covered hook. Pin and catchstitch to lamé cover. Secure gold fabric flower on each side of covered hook on top of stiffened lamé leaves.

METALLIC THREAD

Metallic thread can be plain, multicoloured, gold or silver. It consists of fibres of metallic thread wrapped around a nylon or cotton core. Any friction causes these outer fabrics to wear away, so always hand wind metallic threads on to your bobbin, and use a looser top tension when working with them. Metallic threads are ideal for topstitching lamé, but for doing ordinary seams on lamé fabrics use a matching colour polyester thread.

SILVER CUSHIONS

materials for a pair of cushions

40 cm (15¾ in) and 38 cm (15 in)-square feather cushion pads
1.5 m (59 in) of 115 cm (45 in)-wide silver lamé
1 m (39½ yd) of 115 cm (45 in)-wide gold lamé
2 m (80 in) of 82 cm (32¼ in)-wide iron-on vilene
50 cm (20 in) lightweight polyester wadding
25 cm (10 in) silver grey metallic zip
31 cm (12 in) silver grey metallic zip
1.5 m (59 in) of no. 4 (medium) piping cord
1.8 m (70 in) of no. 5 (large) piping cord
4 polystyrene balls on wires, 2 cm (¾ in) diameter (for antennae), sprayed silver
4 small strips of 3 mm (¹⁄₁₆ in)-wide ribbon (any colour)
matching thread (gold, silver grey)
centimetre pattern paper
scissors, pencil, ballpoint pen, zipper foot

---

to make

1 Cut a 70 cm (27½ in) square of gold lamé and a 60 cm (23½ in) square of silver lamé, plus same-sized vilene squares. Fuse vilene to lamé.
2 The piping for each cushion is made up from bias strips cut diagonally from narrow lengths of gold lamé. To make

the strips, fold down a corner of your piping fabric so that edges are at right angles (90°). Press the fold line, then unfold fabric. Mark 4 cm (1½ in) strips with ballpoint pen parallel to the fold line. Cut, then join strips on the straight grain with 6 mm (¼ in) turnings, making two 1.8 m (70 in) strips. Press.

3 Transfer the diagrams to centimetre pattern paper. Using these as your patterns and turning each wing pattern at fold for 1 butterfly, cut:

FOR THE 40 CM (15¾ IN) CUSHION

from gold lamé 2 large butterflies from fused square
from silver lamé 2 × 41 cm (16 in) squares, 2 antennae strips 12 cm (4¾ in) × 2.5 cm (1 in) from fused square, 2 medium butterflies from fused square
from wadding 1 large and 1 medium butterfly shape
from vilene 2 × 40 cm (15¾ in) squares

FOR THE 38 CM (15 IN) CUSHION

from gold lamé 2 medium butterflies from fused square
from silver lamé 2 × 38 cm (15 in) squares, 2 antennae strips 12 cm (4¾ in) × 2.5 cm (1 in) from fused square, 2 small butterflies from fused square
from wadding 1 medium and 1 small butterfly shape
from vilene 2 × 38 cm (15 in) squares.

NOTE Small notches mark openings on outer edges of wings.

4 Place the shiny side of the vilene to the wrong side of each lamé cushion square. Press with a warm dry iron to fuse.

5 Using a ballpoint pen, draw swirls (see photograph) on the vilene side of each front butterfly. Using the matching thread, topstitch the swirls on the vilene sides.

6 Place wadding butterfly to vilene side of four front butterflies. Pin and tack. Place lamé sides of each butterfly together and, with 6 mm (¼ in) turnings, pin, tack and machine stitch round butterfly shape, leaving marked opening between notches. Remove tacking. Trim corners and turn through opening. Push out points of wings. Tuck turnings back into butterfly and catchstitch together to close. Tack a line 1 cm (⅜ in) from edge of butterfly. Topstitch 2 mm (¹⁄₁₆ in) from edge. Remove tack-

ing. With swirled wing in front, join large and medium butterfly and then join medium and small butterfly. Pleat centres and catchstitch to hold.

7 Place piping cord inside lamé bias strips with wrong sides together. Pin, tack and using zipper foot, machine stitch close to cord. Remove tacking. Trim flat edges to 1 cm (⅜ in).

8 Starting from centre of one side of one cushion square and leaving 5 cm (2 in) of piping free, pin, tack and machine stitch along edges over previous stitching on piping. Snip flat edge of piping at corners to ease. Overlap and bind 3 cm (1¼ in) of cord at meeting point, join bias strip with 3 mm (⅛ in) turnings and re-cover cord. Continue machine stitch line. Remove all tacking. Repeat for second cushion.

9 Open zip. With zip face down, position centrally on piping turnings on one side of cover. Pin, tack and machine stitch using zipper foot. Remove tacking. With right side of cushion squares together, pin and tack from the beginning of zip, along three remaining sides, to end of zip. Machine stitch with 1 cm (⅜ in) seam allowance, pressing zipper foot as close to piping as possible. Repeat for second cushion.

10 Keeping zip open, match second side of zip to remaining raw edge of other square. Pin, tack and machine stitch. Remove tacking. Trim all seams and corners. Turn cover to right side through open zip, pushing out piped corners. If original stitching on piping is visible, turn cushion to wrong side and machine stitch closer to piping. Turn through to right side. Repeat for second cushion.

11 With right sides together, fold one 12 cm (4¾ in) antenna strip of vilene-backed silver lamé in half lengthways, wrapping round 2 mm (¹⁄₁₆ in) strip of ribbon. Pin, tack and machine stitch across short end, catching in the ribbon. Avoiding ribbon, stitch down long edge 6 mm (¼ in) from folded side. Trim seam. Holding stitched short end, pull rouleau through gently. Trim away ribbon. Repeat for remaining antennae. Slide tubing on to wire of ball decorations.

12 Arrange ends of tubing under assembled butterflies. Catchstitch antennae and then butterflies to top right hand corners of cushion covers.

13 Insert cushions in covers.

FUSING LAMÉ WITH VILENE

Lamé has quite a loose weave. When you fuse it to vilene you may find that the adhesive webbing melts through to the right side of the lamé and leaves a small sticky deposit on the iron and ironing board. To prevent this happening, sandwich the lamé and vilene pieces between two pressing cloths (dampened, and then squeezed out well) before you fuse them together with your iron.

Scale 1 square = 5 cm (approx 2 in)

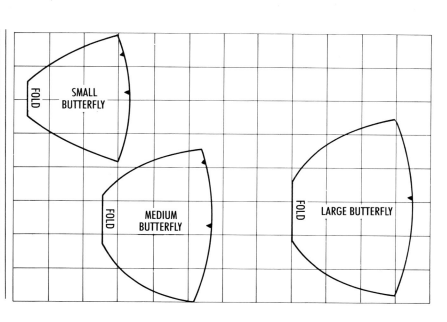

FOLD SMALL BUTTERFLY

FOLD MEDIUM BUTTERFLY

FOLD LARGE BUTTERFLY

RUBY PHOTO-FRAMES

Celebrate a ruby wedding anniversary with these elegant red lamé photo-frames padded and decorated with simple 'fans' of matching red lamé in the corner. Capture some of the treasured moments in the marriage or make a mirror in the same way. Use the cutting out pattern provided for both frames, but on the large frame work to 5cm (2in) per square and on the small frame 4cm (1½in) per square.

LARGE FRAME

materials

25 cm (10 in) of 115 cm (45 in)-wide ruby red lamé
46 cm (18 in) × 18 cm (7 in) piece of cardboard
20 cm (8 in) length of 100 cm (39½ in)-wide lightweight polyester wadding
bondaweb
card-backed metal ring (optional)
matching thread (red)
centimetre pattern paper
fabric adhesive, pencil, ruler, scissors

to make

1 Transfer the diagrams to the centimetre pattern paper. Using these as your patterns, cut the following:
from lamé 1 front frame 'A' (add 1.5cm/⅝in turnings, leave centre intact), 2 backs 'B', 2 stand shapes 'E' (add 1.5cm/⅝in turnings), 2 oblongs each 17cm (6½in) × 7cm (2¾in), 1 frame backing 'C'
from wadding 1 front frame 'A' with 1.5cm (⅝in) turnings removed on each outer edge (remove the centre section after applying adhesive)
from bondaweb 1 × 8.5cm (3¼in) square, 1 oblong 17cm (6½in) × 7cm (2¾in)
from cardboard 1 front frame 'C', 1 back 'D', 1 stand 'E' (scored as indicated).
2 Using a warm dry iron, fuse the bondaweb square to the centre of the wrong side of lamé front frame 'A', keeping paper backing intact.
3 Apply adhesive to front of cardboard front frame 'C'. Leave to become tacky. Glue polyester wadding piece 'A' to front frame 'C'. When dry, snip into the

centre of the wadding square, leaving 1cm (⅜in) on all four inside edges.
4 Apply adhesive to back side of cardboard front frame 'C'. Leave to become tacky. Glue wrong side of lamé frame backing 'C' centrally on back of card frame.
5 Position lamé-covered bondaweb square with paper side to wadding covered frame. Lightly tack round lamé front frame to hold in place.
6 Working from the front, carefully snip through lamé and bondaweb into corners of centre square. Stop approximately 3mm (⅛in) short of the exact corner. Peel off the bondaweb paper, one corner at a time and press back on to lamé frame backing 'C', pulling evenly. Catchstitch the edges to hold in position. Repeat for the remaining three sides.
7 Wrap the 1.5cm (⅝in) outside turnings on the front lamé frame round to the frame backing 'C'. Pin and catchstitch to hold in position. Pulling firmly, fold the corners and smooth away any tucks on the padded frame.
8 With right sides of lamé frame backs 'B' together and with 1.5cm (⅝in) turnings, pin, tack and machine stitch along three sides.
With right sides of lamé stands 'E'

together and with 6mm (¼in) turnings, pin, tack and machine stitch along three sides, leaving base open. Remove tacking.
9 Trim turnings on stand and back. Carefully turn both through and slide in cardboard square (D) and cardboard stand 'E'. (It must fit precisely. If 'pocket' is slightly baggy, turn back to wrong side and machine stitch inside original row.) Catchstitch open edges securely to close.
10 Position scored oblong at top of stand to exact centre of covered back, with bottom edge of stand level with bottom edge of frame. Catchstitch stand securely to frame back.
(For wall hanging, use a strong adhesive to secure card-backed metal ring in a position 1.5cm (⅝in) below top of frame.)
11 Fuse lamé oblongs together with bondaweb. Pleat the length to form a 'fan' effect. Catchstitch just above bottom edge to hold fan shape. Pin to top right-hand corner, open fan, and catchstitch to secure.

Scale 1 square = 5/4 cm (approx 2/1½ in)

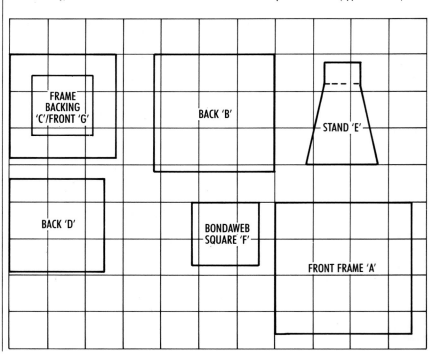

SMALL FRAME

materials

25 cm (10 in) of 115 cm (45 in)-wide ruby red lamé

38 cm (15 in) × 14 cm (5½ in) piece of cardboard

20 cm (8 in) length of 100 cm (39½ in)-wide lightweight polyester wadding

bondaweb

matching thread (red)

centimetre pattern paper

fabric adhesive, pencil, ruler, scissors

to make

1 Transfer the diagrams to centimetre pattern paper. Using these as your patterns, cut the following:

from lamé 1 front frame 'A' (with 1.5 cm/⅝ in) turnings, leave centre intact), 2 backs 'B', 2 stand shapes 'E' (with 1.5 cm/⅝ in turnings), 2 oblongs each 17 cm (6½ in) × 5 cm (2 in)

from cardboard 1 front frame 'C', 1 back 'D', 1 stand 'E' (scored and trimmed as indicated)

from wadding 1 front frame 'A' with 1.5 cm (⅝ in) turnings removed on outer edges (remove centre section after applying adhesive)

from bondaweb 1 × 9 cm (3½ in) square, 1 oblong 17 cm (6½ in) × 5 cm (2 in).

2 To assemble the small frame, follow Steps 2-11 of the large frame.

FRAMES FOR OTHER OCCASIONS

The simple shape of these photo-frames lends itself to a variety of fabrics. For other wedding anniversaries, cover the frame with gold or silver lamé, or crisp white cotton and decorate the corner with a group of crystals. Make them into a Christmas present, using a holly print, a tartan with some red baubles, or a simple red or green lawn finished off with fruits, and sprayed seed heads.

PEARL SEQUIN CUSHION

This simple 'envelope' of white taffeta makes an unusual gift for a pearl wedding anniversary. The flap opens out to reveal a covering of 'pearl' beads and sequins, while a large 'pearl' drop bead is used to secure the flap closed. It could easily be used as a present for a special bride, or made in a different coloured fabric and decorated to be suitable for a number of other special celebrations.

materials

1 feather cushion pad 35 cm (13¾ in) × 22 cm (8½ in)
50 cm (20 in) of 115 cm (45 in)-wide cream polyester taffeta
25 cm (10 in) cream zip
1 box each of: tiny pearl stars, large pearl stars, small round pearl sequins, large round pearl sequins
3 cm (1¼ in) pearl drop bead
matching thread (cream)
centimetre pattern paper
scissors, ruler, pencil, tailor's chalk, zipper foot

to make

1 Transfer the diagrams to the centimetre pattern paper. Using these as your pattern, cut the following:
from taffeta 2 oblongs, 4 flaps.
2 With right sides of two flap pieces facing, match raw edges and take 1 cm (⅜ in) turnings. Pin, tack and machine stitch short sides of flaps together leaving two long straight sides open. Turn through to right side, trimming off point of flap. Press lightly. Repeat for other flap.
3 Slide hand into one turned flap. Working the needle from under the flap in this way, sew on sequins, stars and pearls at random. Leave 1.5 cm (⅝ in) of the straight unstitched edge of flap free of sequins to prevent sewing over them when joining flap to oblong. When the flap is covered, pin and tack along the edges to hold the shape flat.
4 Sandwich the undecorated flap between two right sides of two taffeta oblongs. Pin and tack across one long side of oblong, matching raw edges and taking 1 cm (⅜ in) turnings. Lightly press tacked seam open.

5 With right side of zip to pressed seam, pin and tack zip between opening notches. Using zipper foot and working on right side of cushion pieces, slide head of zip past zipper foot and topstitch all round zip. Remove tacking. Open zip.
6 Take plain flap over on to one oblong, but **not** covering zip. Pin and tack to oblong along the pointed edges of the flap.
7 Sandwich decorated flap between the two oblongs. Place sequin side down on to the oblong with undecorated tacked flap. Check to ensure that

Scale 1 square = 5 cm (approx 2 in)

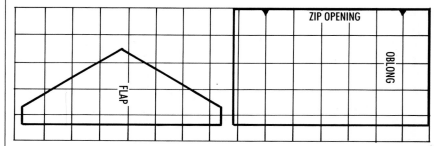

zip is open. Match remaining three sides of cushion and straight edge of decorated flap. Pin, tack and machine stitch with 1 cm (⅜ in) turnings.
8 Remove all tacking and trim corners. Turn through open zip. Push out corners neatly. Remove tacking on plain flap, which will probably release a slight tension. Slide cushion pad into taffeta cover. Allow flap to re-settle in new position. Pin, tack and catchstitch the point, keeping hand over pad inside taffeta cover. Sew pearl drop bead to point of plain flap.
9 Work a thread chain on decorated flap point, starting approximately 1 cm (⅜ in) on seam from point. Work a 2.5 cm (1 in) chain and secure it firmly 1 cm (⅜ in) from point. Stand pearl drop bead up and slide chain over it to close the 'envelope'.

CRYSTAL SERVIETTE SET

Sparkling crystals decorate these deli-cate cotton Victoria lawn napkins and matching napkin rings. A set of three packed in white tissue in a beautiful gift box makes an ideal gift for a crystal anniversary. The crisp bridal white means that they could also be a thoughtful present for a new bride, or they could be made in 'gold', 'silver' or 'ruby' red for other anniversaries.

materials for set of 3

1 m (39½ in) of 1 m (39½ in)-wide Victoria lawn
10 cm (4 in) of 1 m (39½ in)-wide lightweight polyester wadding
13.5 cm (5¼ in) of 2 cm (¾ in)-wide white velcro
approx. 18 pear-shaped crystals
matching thread (white)
centimetre pattern paper
scissors, pencil, ruler

to make

1 Transfer the diagrams to the centi-metre pattern paper. Using these as your pattern, cut the following:
from Victoria lawn 3 serviette squares, 6 serviette ring strips
from wadding 3 serviette ring strips
from velcro 3 × 4.5 cm (1¾ in) lengths.
2 Tear apart one 4.5 cm (1¾ in) length of velcro and position hook piece on right side of one lawn strip, as diagram. Pin, tack and machine stitch. Position corresponding loop half to right side of second strip of lawn, as diagram. Pin, tack and machine stitch. Remove tack-ing. Repeat for remaining strips.
3 Pin and tack wadding strips to wrong sides of three lawn strips.
4 With right sides together and hook and loop piece at opposite ends, match raw edges and take 1 cm (⅜ in) turn-ings. Pin, tack and machine stitch be-tween notches. Trim corners, turn through opening. Push out corners. Slide turnings on opening to inside and catchstitch together. Press. Decorate outside the centre with the crystals. Repeat to complete all the other servi-ette rings.
5 To make the serviettes, turn a 1 cm (⅜ in) hem to wrong side on all four edges of one lawn square. Pin, tack and machine stitch. Remove tacking. Press. Working on wrong side of lawn, fold a 5 cm (2 in) hem on to the right side along each edge. Form a mitre on each corner by bringing the corner edges up together, creating a line from inner hem edges out to pointed corner. Pin, tack and machine stitch, taking 1 cm (⅜ in) turnings. Remove tacking. Trim mitre seam down to 3 mm (⅛ in). Press seam open. Repeat for other corners. Carefully turn each mitred corner through to right side, pointing corners out to form a 5 cm (2 in) hem. Lightly steam press. Pin and tack along inner hem edge and folded edge to hold. Topstitch, working from wrong side of serviette 2 mm (¹⁄₁₆ in) from inner hem edge. Remove tacking. Arrange crystals in corners as photograph and sew in position. Repeat for other serviettes.

Scale 1 square = 5 cm (approx 2 in)

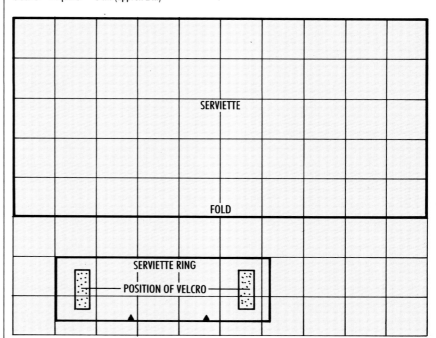

PAPER DOVE BASKET

This pretty white basket can be used to hold a variety of small presents to celebrate the paper anniversary: two years of marriage. Tiny gifts can be hidden in the miniature baskets and small boxes to surprise the receiver. The larger basket is lined with doilies and decorated with satin ribbons and paper doves.

materials

child's wicker shopping basket
2 miniature shopping baskets
white aerosol spray paint
white card
2 m (2¼ yds) of 6 mm (¼ in)-wide white double satin ribbon
2 white paper doilies
2 sheets of jeweller's white tissue paper
oblong pill boxes (from chemist's)
centimetre pattern paper
small piece of card (to fit pattern)
scissors, pencil

to make

1 Spray two or three coats of matt white paint on the child's basket and the two miniature baskets. Leave to dry.
2 Transfer the bird diagram to centimetre paper, and then to the small piece of card. Using this as your pattern, cut five shapes from white card.
3 Fold the sheets of tissue paper into an oblong, then form a concertina shape. Using sharp scissors, cut the tissue into thin strips.
4 Place doilies in large basket, folding frilled edges over each end of basket. Sprinkle shredded tissue lightly on top of doilies and use it to line the boxes and miniature baskets. Fill boxes and small baskets with tiny gifts to put in the large basket.
5 Wind 1 m (1⅛ yd) of the satin ribbon round handle of large basket. Finish the ends with bows.
6 Make a slit in three birds (see photograph) and slide a length of ribbon 31 cm (12 in) long through each slit. Knot end of ribbon or tie a bow. Tie the other end to the basket handles.
7 Glue remaining birds to small boxes. Decorate with ribbon. Fill boxes with gifts and arrange in main basket.

MORE CARDBOARD SHAPES

The dove used in the project here is just one of a number of shapes with which you could decorate the basket. A butterfly, a leaf or a fish would all look equally effective. Cut them out from cardboard in varying shades of pastel, and tie on matching ribbons.

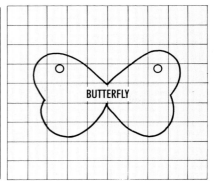

BUTTERFLY

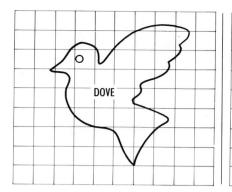

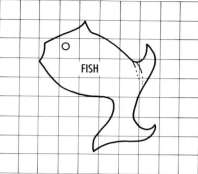

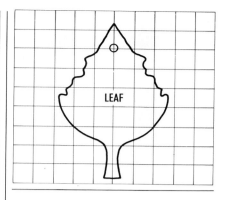

MAKING A BOX

Try making your own little cardboard boxes to go in the basket. Cut out the shape below, increasing the size proportionately as desired. Make folds along all the dotted lines and then cut along lines AB, CD and EF. Pull up flap G and glue to the bottom edge of the bottom square to give your basic box shape. Fold in the side flaps and finally fold in the two remaining sides of the cube. The box is finished.

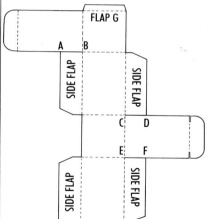

GIFT BOX DECORATIONS

To decorate your boxes, try covering them with some gift wrapping paper after you have cut out the box shape from card, but before you assemble it. Alternatively cut motifs out of some wrapping paper and glue these to the box. Other possible decorations are sequins, for a glittery look or shapes cut out from paper doilies, for a lacey finish.

ANIMAL BIRTHDAYS

Finding suitable presents in the shops for pets is never easy, if you want to avoid edible goods. Here are some ideas: simple gifts for a dog, a cat or a bird in a cage. The reversible dog coat can be worn in any weather: one side is in practical bright red cotton-backed PVC with tiny black Scottie dogs appliquéd on to one corner. This is the wet weather option. The reverse side of the dog coat is cosy black cotton quilting, specially chosen to keep out the cold. A matching red cotton towel, edged with black bias binding and decorated with the same Scottie motif is easy to make and will come in handy after wet and muddy walks.

For feline companions, make a round cat mat. Big enough to take both food and drink bowls, this will help keep the kitchen floor clean and dry. The round PVC cloth is decorated with tiny velcro paw prints. A family of little grey mice, made with felt, pipe-cleaners and scraps of wadding adhere to the paw prints, giving the cat something to play with after the meal.

Celebrate a budgie's birthday with a bird cage cover. Made in bright yellow and pink felt, it is cleverly designed to look like a small house with two windows, windowboxes full of flowers, and a doorway – much more attractive then having an old cloth draped over the cage to keep out the light in the evening.

in this chapter

Right Some unusual but easily made presents for a pet dog and cat. The smart black and red dog coat lies on the floor, ready for its owner to wear on a wet or windy walk, and the matching towel rests on the kitchen cupboards behind. The cat's gift – a yellow mat for feeding time – is already being used.

Left A detail of the decorations on the felt bird cage cover, made to represent a little house with windowboxes full of flowers.

DOG COAT AND TOWEL

The best-dressed dog in the park will stay warm and dry wearing this smart reversible coat. Made in prequilted polycotton fabric backed with bright waterproof PVC, the coat is bound with contrasting cotton bias binding. The large luxurious towel, also bound in cotton bias binding and trimmed with Scotties, will dry even the biggest dog.

QUILTED COAT

materials

50 cm (20 in) of 115 cm (45 in)-wide ready-quilted black polyester/cotton
50 cm (20 in) of 150 cm (59 in)-wide red cotton-backed PVC
2.5 m (2¾ yd) of 2.5 cm (1 in)-wide scarlet cotton bias binding
scrap of red polyester/cotton, 36 cm (14 in) × 6 cm (2⅜ in) for strap
scrap of black cotton-backed PVC
48 cm (19 in) of 2 cm (¾ in)-wide black velcro
matching thread (red, black)
centimetre pattern paper
red wool for 3 pom-pons
card to make pom-pons
teflon foot, tailor's chalk, scissors, pencil, ruler, sellotape

to make

1 Transfer the diagrams to centimetre pattern paper. Using these as patterns, cut the following:
from black quilted fabric 1 coat shape, 1 strap
from red PVC 1 coat shape
from red polyester/cotton 1 strap
from black PVC 1 dog motif
from bias binding 1 × 96 cm (37½ in) length, 1 × 1.5 m (59 in) length.
2 Position dog motif on right-hand of red PVC coat shape. Sellotape to hold. Using teflon foot, topstitch 2 mm (1/16 in) from edges. Remove sellotape.
3 Cut velcro into four equal 12 cm (4¾ in) strips. Position velcro halves as shown on diagram, 2 loop pieces on the quilted coat shape and 2 on PVC coat shape. Position 2 hook pieces on the red strap piece, one on each end. Pin, tack and machine stitch. Remove tacking.

4 With wadding side of quilted coat shape to cotton side of PVC coat shape, pin and tack, taking 6 mm (¼ in) turnings.
5 With right sides of the quilted black strap and red strap facing and working from notch to notch, pin, tack and machine stitch with 6 mm (¼ in) turnings. Remove tacking. Trim corners. Turn through notched opening. Roll seams out with fingertips. Pin and tack, tucking in seams at opening. Topstitch, using black or red thread, 2 mm (1/16 in) from edges. Remove tacking.
6 Open out the 1.5 m (59 in) length of bias binding. With right sides matching, place raw edge of binding to raw edge of PVC coat shape. Beginning at neck edge and working along the 1 cm (⅜ in) crease, pin, tack and machine stitch, using red thread. Remove tacking. Fold remaining half of binding over raw edge. Pin, tack and catchstitch to quilted coat shape.
7 Find the centre of the 96 cm (37½ in) length of bias binding. Position at centre back notch. Repeat as for binding coat shape. Once bias is attached to

Scale 1 square = 5 cm (approx 2 in)

WORKING WITH TOWELLING

To prevent the underside of the towelling catching on the metal teeth of the machine, place a sheet of tissue paper under the fabric, or use a roller foot or no-snag foot. Sew with a medium to large needle, 100% polyester thread and a long stitch length.

neck shape, topstitch closely across short ends and along edges to neck. Remove tacking.
8 Make three pom-pons 4 cm (1½ in) in diameter, leaving a length of wool 12 cm (4¾ in) long on each (see pages 62–3). Fold the long piece of wool four times and catchstitch or knot at each pom-pon to make a thick loose cord. Group the three pom-pons at centre back. Catchstitch them to the edge of the binding so that they reverse easily.

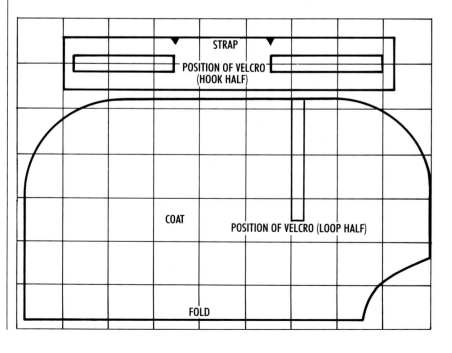

100

DOG TOWEL

materials

90 cm (36 in) of 90 cm (36 in)-wide red cotton
    towelling
3 m (3¼ yd) of 2.5 cm (1 in)-wide black cotton
    bias binding
40 cm (15¾ in) × 15 cm (6 in) of black
    polyester/cotton fabric
40 cm (15¾ in) × 15 cm (6 in) of bondaweb
centimetre pattern paper
thick card
tailor's chalk, scissors, pencil, ruler

to make

1 Transfer the diagrams to centimetre
pattern paper and then the dog motif
pattern to a piece of thick card.
2 Trim the 90cm (36 in) piece of
towelling to form a true square. To
curve the corners, place the corner
pattern, in turn, on each corner edge.
Mark with tailor's chalk and trim away
crescent piece.
3 Position the folded binding around
the raw edge of towelling square. Beginning at the centre of one side, pin
and tack the binding to towel, curving
evenly round each corner. Be sure to
catch both edges of binding into tacking
stitches. Do not tack the binding 10cm
(4 in) either side of the meeting point.

Open out binding and join the short
edges with a 6mm (¼ in) seam. Re-fold
binding again over remaining raw edge
of towelling. Pin and tack. Topstitch on
extreme inner edge of folded binding.
Make sure that both sides of the binding
have been caught in the stitching. Press
lightly.
4 Using a warm dry iron, fuse the
polyester/cotton oblong to the same
size oblong of bondaweb. Working on
the paper side of the bondaweb and
using the card pattern of the Scottie
dog, mark two left and two right dogs.
Peel off paper backing. Fuse corresponding shapes together. Position a
Scottie dog shape in each of the two
opposite corners. Catchstitch the motif
in place to hold.

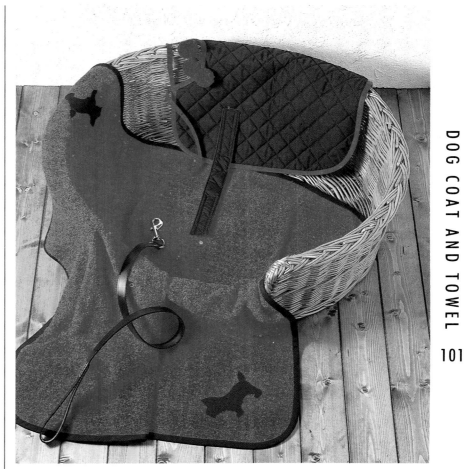

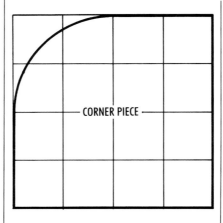

CORNER PIECE

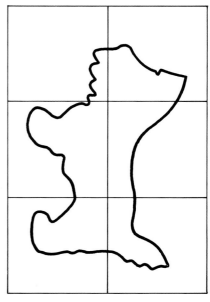

Scale 1 square = 5cm (approx 2 in)

CAT MAT

Not only will this bright practical feeding mat protect the kitchen floor – it will also provide hours of cat fun with the family of detachable felt mice who live on it! The wipe-clean mat is bound with cotton bias binding in a contrasting colour and the mice are attached to cat 'paw pads' made from velcro circles. Stuffing the mice with a little catmint will making the toys even more appealing to their new owner.

materials

MAT

55 cm (21½ in) of 150 cm (59 in)-wide cotton-backed PVC
55 cm (21½ in) of 82 cm (32¼ in)-wide craft-quality vilene
2 m (2¼ yd) of 2.5 cm (1 in)-wide yellow cotton bias binding
matching thread (yellow)

THREE MICE

2 × 22 cm (8½ in) squares grey felt
3 long grey chenille pipecleaners
scraps of wadding
6 small beads
whiskers
27 cm (10½ in) of 2 cm (¾ in)-wide grey velcro
matching thread (grey)
centimetre pattern paper
scissors, pencil, rubber

to make

1 Transfer the diagrams to centimetre pattern paper. Place the quarter-circle pattern four times to create a circle. Using these as your patterns, cut the following:
from PVC 2 mat circles
from vilene 1 mat circle
from grey felt 6 mouse sides, 3 mouse bases, 6 ears
from velcro 12 small pads, 3 large centre pads
2 Tear apart the velcro pads. Position the small velcro hook circle pads round one large centre 'pad' on the right side of one PVC mat circle, using the photograph as a guide. Pin, tack and machine stitch. Remove tacking and repeat for the other paw marks.
3 Position the vilene circle between

cotton-backed sides of the two PVC circles. Pin and tack to hold.
4 Wrap the folded bias binding over the edge of the mat evenly. Pin, tack and topstitch as close as possible to the inside edge of binding. Overlap end on bias turning 2 mm (1/16 in) to inside of binding. Catchstitch to neaten. Remove tacking.
5 To make the mice, position a 2.5 cm (1 in) velcro loop oblong along felt base of one mouse body. Pin, tack and machine stitch. Repeat for other mice. Remove tacking.
6 Curl one end of the chenille pipecleaner tail. Position straight end on centre back of grey felt base. Catchstitch. Repeat for the other remaining base pieces.
7 Join two curved body pieces along centre back with 6 mm (¼ in) turnings. Pin, tack and machine stitch. Repeat for other mice body pieces. Remove tacking.
8 Carefully tucking tail away from machine line, place right sides of joined backs to velcro side of base. Leave the 4.5 cm (1¾ in) opening and take 6 mm

Scale 1 square = 5 cm (approx 2 in)

(¼ in) turnings. Tack, machine stitch. Remove tacking. Turn body with tail through to the right side. Repeat for other mice.
9 Working through the 4.5 cm (1¾ in) opening, fill the mouse body with scraps of wadding. Catchstitch the opening together, tucking turnings to inside. Repeat for other mice.
10 Fold ears lengthways and position one on each side of head. Pin, tack and catchstitch, keeping ears upright. Sew on beads for eyes. Repeat for other mice.
11 Thread whiskers in needle and pull through four. Knot each whisker on side of face. Repeat for other mice. Match velcro on mouse base to paw prints – all ready for a game!

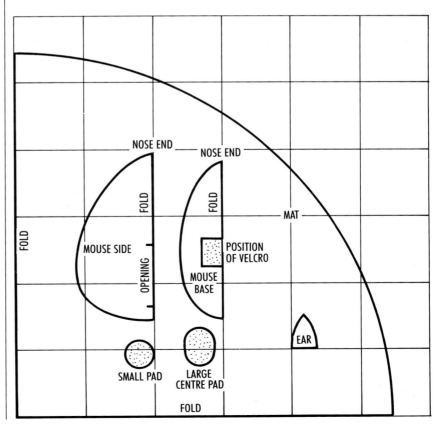

BIRD CAGE COVER

A warm snug house to slip over the cage of your pet bird, this cage is a 'caravan' shape measuring 35cm (13¾in) high, 43cm (17in) long and 28cm (11in) wide.

materials

- 1.2 m (1⅓ yd) of 183 cm (72 in)-wide buttercup yellow felt
- 1.2 m (1⅓ yd) of 90 cm (36 in)-wide polyester/cotton print
- 15 cm (6 in) of 183 cm (72 in)-wide cyclamen pink felt
- 2.5 m (2¾ yd) of no. 3 cotton piping cord
- 22 cm (8½ in) square of turquoise felt
- 2 × 22 cm (8½ in) squares of hyacinth blue felt
- 22 cm (8½ in) square of lime green felt
- 2 blue, 2 yellow, 2 pink acrylic pom-pons, 2 cm (¾ in) in diameter
- 3 pink, 1 blue, 1 yellow acrylic pom-pons, 1 cm (⅜ in) in diameter
- matching thread (pink, yellow)
- bondaweb
- centimetre pattern paper
- pencil, sharp pointed scissors
- adhesive, zipper foot

to make

1 Transfer the diagrams to centimetre pattern paper. Using these as your patterns, cut the following:

from yellow felt 1 front cage piece cut on fold, 2 back cage pieces cut along dotted line, 2 oblongs (roof/sides) each 56cm (22 in) × 29cm (11½ in). Mark a 12cm (4¾ in) opening on each short edge, 8.5 cm (3¼ in) in from long sides

from polyester/cotton 1 front cage piece cut on fold, 2 back cage pieces cut along dotted line, 2 oblongs each 56cm (22 in) × 29cm (11½ in), 2 left and 2 right curtain shapes

from pink felt 2.5m (2¾ yd) × 5cm (2 in) strip for piping (joined on short ends), 2 windows, 10 strips of tiles for roof

from blue felt 1 door, 2 window box backings

from turquoise felt 4 front door panels, 2 window boxes

from lime green felt stalks, leaves and grass.

2 Turn, tack and press 1 cm (⅜ in) to wrong side down centre back cage

pieces of polyester/cotton lining and yellow felt.

3 Place the piping cord along centre of pink felt piping strip. Pin and tack felt over cord. Using a zipper foot, machine stitch close to cord along the full length.

4 Match short ends of yellow felt roof/side oblongs. Taking 1cm (⅜ in) turnings, pin, tack and machine stitch from the edge to the notch on each side to leave a 12cm (4¾ in) handle opening. Remove tacking. Press seam and turnings on opening to wrong side. Tack to hold open. Repeat for polyester/cotton lining oblongs.

5 Position straight edge of first line of scalloped tiles on double notches on joined yellow felt roof/sides oblong. Pin, tack and machine stitch along straight edge. Working upwards towards the handle opening, add the remaining four strips, alternating curves to form a 'fish scale' effect. Repeat for other half of roof. Remove any visible tacking.

6 Cut 28cm (11 in) off the 2.5m (2¾ yd) length of felt piping. Open out the turnings. Pin, tack and topstitch flattened piping strip to cover centre roof seam line. Mark the 12cm (4¾ in)

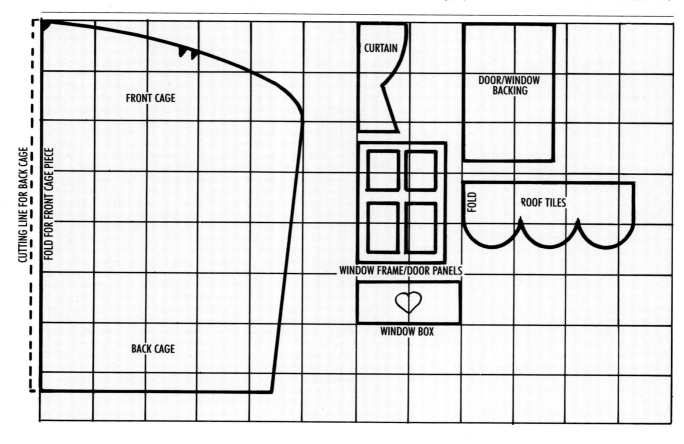

handle opening centrally on one side, close to the machine line. Using the scissors, cut along handle opening line. Matching slit to tacked opening on felt, pin, tack and machine stitch a 'letter box' oblong around the opening of all four sides.

7 Trim turnings on remaining felt piping length to 1cm (⅜in). Match raw edges of piping to raw edge of one long side of roof/side oblong. Pin and tack to hold. If piping distorts the ridge piping at hem edge, cut off a small amount of cord from each end of the ridge using sharp scissors. Repeat for other side.

8 With curved side of front cage piece to felt piping and right sides facing, match piping ridge to centre notch on felt front. Pin and tack. Using zipper foot, machine stitch seam all around. Remove tacking.

9 Position folded tacked centre back seam on back felt cage on piping ridge. Match curve on back pieces to piping. With right sides facing, pin and tack. Using zipper foot, machine stitch through all layers. Remove tacking.

10 Join polyester/cotton front and back cage linings to roof/side oblong linings

leaving handle opening as for cover. Turn 1cm (⅜in) hem to wrong side along base edge. Pin and tack.

11 Trim base edge of felt cage cover level. Remove 1cm (⅜in) of piping cord from ends of covered piping, so that the felt casing can be turned with the hem easily. Turn under a 1cm (⅜in) hem to wrong side and tack.

With wrong side of lining to wrong side of felt cage cover, match seams, edges and handle openings. Pin and tack along seams, smoothing shapes down together. Catchstitch lining to felt cover down centre back edges around

WORKING WITH FELT

Felt is one of the most versatile fabrics available for craft work today. Coming in an enormous range of colours, it is easy to cut out as it doesn't fray. However, as it is a composition cloth made from rolling and pressing wool with lees (wine sediment) or size, it is not that durable.

handle opening and along base edge. Remove tacking.

12 Cut out heart shapes from both turquoise window box oblongs carefully. (They will be used to decorate the centre of the window frames.) Apply bondaweb to one side of each of the following pieces:

3 blue felt oblongs (2 window backings, 1 door), 2 pink felt window frames, 4 printed cotton curtain shapes (2 left, 2 right), 2 turquoise window boxes, 4 turquoise door panels, fused to one side of the door.

13 Slide finished cage cover over one end of the ironing board. With felt side uppermost, assemble the bondaweb-backed pieces, positioning them as indicated on the pattern. Fuse to front of cover in this order:

2 blue window backings, left and right curtains (matching top edges), pink window frames, flower box oblongs to bottom edge of window frames, door.

14 Using fabric adhesive, position the hearts, stalks, leaves and large pompons on windows, and around door, using small pom-pons.

CHRISTMAS

Christmas is a time when everyone wants to join in with making decorations for the house and the dining table. The good news is that, even if you're new to handicrafts, there are plenty of simple things to try out.

Start off the festive season with an Advent calendar for the kids. Instead of buying the usual cardboard one from the shops, make a more spectacular and colourful version of your own from felt. There are two different designs: the Advent tree made from green felt and covered with 24 pockets in the shapes of parcels and hearts; and the Advent Snowman – white felt covered with colourful robins, Christmas puddings and trees, holly leaves and parcels.

As Christmas approaches, make a decoration for the front door: a gorgeous dark green taffeta ring, adorned with tinsel, mini-crackers, strings of red and gold beads, holly, berries and fir cones sprayed with gold paint.

A set of place mats, coasters and serviette rings made from red and green berry print PVC is ideal for creating a festive atmosphere at informal holiday meals in the kitchen. From the same material, make an apron for the hard-working cook.

The dining table on Christmas Day deserves special treatment. Dress it up with a pure white cotton voile tablecloth and serviettes decorated with appliquéd christmas trees.

Right An impressive array of gifts and decorations for the family over Christmas. The Christmas door decoration and felt Advent tree hang on the wall, and you can just see the Christmas table set – mats, coasters and serviette rings made from a green and red berry print – on the sideboard below. Serviettes which go with the white cotton voile tablecloth are arranged on the table to show off the delicate appliquéd Christmas trees.

Left A detail of the snowman advent calendar, showing pockets made in the shape of a robin, Christmas tree and Christmas pudding.

ADVENT TREE

Hang up this big felt tree on the first day of December and discover a secret tucked inside a heart or parcel every day until Christmas! This giant-sized Advent calendar will become a traditional part of the family's celebrations straightaway.

materials

75 cm (29½ in) of 183 cm (72 in)-wide dark green felt

50 cm (20 in) of 115 cm (45 in)-wide Christmas print fabric

1 m (39½ in) of 1 m (39½ in)-wide heavy weight polyester wadding

35 cm (13¾ in) of 115 cm (45 in)-wide red polyester/cotton

25 cm (10 in) of 1 m (39½ in)-wide medium weight polyester wadding

25 cm (10 in) of 1 m (39½ in)-wide lightweight polyester wadding

60 cm (23½ in) square red felt

8 m (8¾ yd) of 1 cm (⅜ in)-wide red double satin ribbon

1.5 m (59 in) of 3 mm (⅛ in)-wide gold Russia braid

70 cm (27½ in) gold elastic thread

matching thread (dark green, bright red, gold)

6 imitation fruits on wire stalks (from florist's)

gold sequin stars, 1.5 cm (⅝ in) wide

centimetre pattern paper

scissors, tailor's chalk

to make

1 Transfer diagrams to the centimetre pattern paper. Using these as your pattern, cut the following:

from green felt 2 tree shapes, 1 with inverted 'V'-shaped quilting lines marked with tailor's chalk

from heavy weight wadding 1 tree shape, 1 flowerpot rim shape

from red felt 2 flowerpot shapes, 1 flowerpot rim shape

from Christmas print 36 hearts

from red polyester/cotton 12 parcels

from medium weight wadding 1 flowerpot shape

from lightweight wadding 18 hearts, 6 parcels

from ribbon 36 × 19 cm (7½ in) lengths, 1 × 68 cm (26¾ in) length

from gold Russia braid 6 × 13 cm (5 in) lengths, 6 × 11.5 cm (4½ in) lengths

TREE

2 Match the heavy weight wadding tree to one felt tree. Pin and tack. Tack chalk lines of inverted 'V' shapes on felt side. Topstitch on chalk lines to quilt and pad. Tap chalk marks away. With top-stitched side to second felt tree shape, pin, tack and machine stitch 1 cm (⅜ in) from edges, starting and finishing at base opening notches. Remove tacking. Snip into corners, turn to right side

Scale 1 square = 5 cm (approx 2 in)

through opening. Lightly steam press. Rolling seam to edge, tack along all eges to hold tree shape flat. Leave tacking until hearts and parcels are positioned, but remove before final pressing.

FLOWERPOT RIM

3 Position heavy weight wadding strip along one long edge of felt rim shape and up to centre. Sandwich wadding by folding felt over. Pin, tack and machine stitch along the long edges 1 cm (⅜ in)

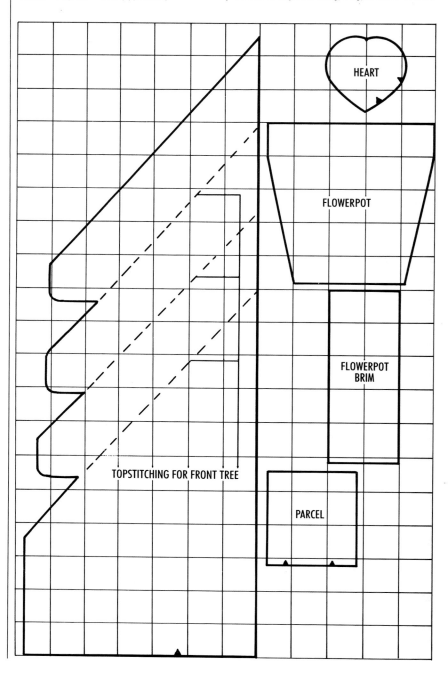

HEART

FLOWERPOT

FLOWERPOT BRIM

TOPSTITCHING FOR FRONT TREE

PARCEL

from the two side edges, pushing wadding towards fold of rim to form an open-ended 'sausage' shape. Snip protruding wadding from side edges.

FLOWERPOT

4 With one red felt flowerpot shape and one medium weight wadding flowerpot shape together, pin and tack round complete shape. With felt side of padded pot shape uppermost, match long raw edges of filled rim to top edge. Pin, tack and machine stitch approximately 6 mm (¼ in) from top edge. With felt sides together, position second pot shape over rimmed pot. Pin, tack and machine stitch 6 mm (¼ in) down sides and across base of pot. Remove tacking. Trim corners. Turn through to right side. Lightly steam press. Slip machined top edge of pot into the 24 cm (9½ in) opening at base of tree, sliding in so that the turned under edges of the tree cover the original 6 mm (¼ in) turnings. Catchstitch pot to front and back of tree, turning in seam allowance on tree opening. Remove visible tacking on flowerpot.

HEARTS

5 With right sides of printed heart shapes together and one lightweight wadding heart shape to one wrong side, pin, tack and machine stitch with 3 mm (⅛ in) seam, leaving the notched 4 cm (1½ in) openings. Turn through opening to right side. Catchstitch opening together. Lightly steam press. Repeat to make 17 more hearts.

6 Take one 19 cm (7½ in)-long piece of ribbon, pin to top centre of one heart, loop over pin and catchstitch across ribbon, leaving the long end free. Remove pins. Repeat for remaining 17 hearts.

PARCELS

7 Arrange long braids down parcel shapes and short braids across parcel shapes. Pin, tack and machine stitch in gold thread along centre of Russia braid. Remove tacking. Place one wadding parcel shape to wrong side of decorated parcel shape, pin and tack. With one red parcel shape to braid/wadding shape and right sides of fabric together, pin, tack and machine stitch 3 mm (⅛ in) from edges, leaving the notched opening at base. Trim corners.

Turn through to right side. Catchstitch opening together. Lightly steam press. Repeat to make five more parcels.

TO FINISH

8 Arrange hearts and parcels on tree as photograph, positioning one heart at the top, then a row of heart/parcel/heart and finally four rows of five each. Pin in position and handsew to tree. Leave top edge of parcels and rounded tops of hearts open for inserting small gifts. Match the remaining 18 lengths of red ribbon, one above each heart, and tack to felt tree, turning 6 mm (¼ in) to neaten, corresponding to ribbons on hearts. Tie bows. Cut ends of ribbon in a slant. Decorate tree with sequin stars at top, on each point, scattered across tree and on some parcels. Add fruits between hearts and parcels, arranging them attractively. Sew stalks in position. Tie the gold elastic thread around base of the tree at top of the pot.

9 Fold the 68 cm (26¾ in) length of ribbon in half and mark with a pin Measure 13 cm (5 in) down each side seam from top point of tree and mark with tailor's chalk. Make a fold 3 cm (1¼ in) deep 13 cm (5 in) from each end of the ribbon and catchstitch the loop securely to each side of tree. Cut slant ends to neaten.

OTHER FABRICS

An advent tree could be made using gold lamé instead of green felt and be given silver lamé pockets. Alternatively make an all white tree covered in sparkling silver stars, or use red and green ginghams for a Scandinavian look.

SNOWMAN ADVENT CALENDAR

Twenty-five pockets to Christmas Eve. Fill the puddings, trees, leaves, robins and parcels with tiny gifts. His carrot nose, lumps of wood for eyes and smart bowler hat make this Snowman authentic enough to be a traditional part of your celebrations.

materials

1.2 m (1⅜ yds) of 90 cm (36 in)-wide white felt
1.2 m (1⅜ yds) of 1 m (39½ in)-wide heavy weight polyester wadding
2 × 22 cm (8½ in) squares of felt in each colour: dark cypress green (holly), light pine green (tree), dark brown (pudding), leather brown (robin)
22 cm (8½ in) square of orange felt
2 × 60 cm (23½ in) squares of felt in each colour: scarlet, black
matching threads (red, green, orange, brown, black, white)
1 m (39½ in) of 3 mm (⅛ in)-wide gold Russia braid
75 cm (29½ in) of 3 mm (⅛ in)-wide green double satin ribbon
2 large cube-shaped black buttons
5 gold star sequins, 15 small red beads, 5 small gold sequins, 25-30 large assorted sequins 1 cm (⅜ in) diameter
centimetre pattern paper
pencil, scissors, fabric adhesive, tissue paper

to make

1 Transfer the diagrams to centimetre pattern paper. Using these as your patterns, cut the following:
from white felt 2 snowman shapes, 5 icings
from dark cypress green felt 10 holly leaves
from light pine green felt 10 Christmas trees
from leather brown felt 10 Christmas puddings
from leather brown felt 10 robins
from scarlet felt 10 parcel shapes, 5 robin breasts, 10 circles 1.5 cm (⅝ in) diameter (holly berries), 2 strips 48 cm (19 in) × 6 cm (2⅜ in) (scarf)
from orange felt 2 carrot shapes (nose)
from black felt 2 hat shapes
from wadding 1 snowman shape, 1 hat shape trimmed on dotted line, 1 48 cm (19 in) × 20 cm (8 in) length for hat brim
from gold Russia braid 5 × 10 cm (4 in) lengths, 5 × 8 cm (3 in) lengths

2 Match pairs of felt parcels, puddings (not icing), robins, trees and holly leaves, topstitch 2 mm (1/16 in) from edge around each pair of shapes to join.
3 Decorate the pockets as follows.

PARCELS

Pin and tack the vertical and then the horizontal lengths of Russia braid to each parcel. Machine stitch through centre of braid to hold. Remove tacking. Decorate each parcel by sewing on one gold star sequin.

CHRISTMAS PUDDINGS

Sew three small red beads to top of icing. Using the adhesive, attach the icing shape to the pudding as in the photograph.

ROBINS

Using the adhesive, attach the breasts to robin shapes. Sew one gold sequin to each robin for eye.

CHRISTMAS TREES

Sew 5 or 6 large round sequins to each Christmas tree.

HOLLY LEAVES

Topstitch two machine lines down centre of each double-thickness holly leaf.

Scale 1 square = 5 cm (approx 2 in)

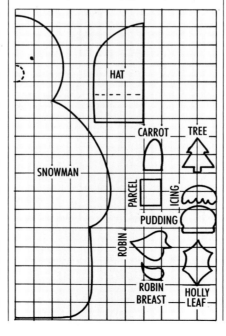

Using the adhesive, glue 2 felt 'berries' to each leaf.

4 Position 24 of the felt shapes on one felt snowman as photograph. Keep back 1 robin for hat decoration. Pin, tack and catchstitch each shape in place, leaving tops open to form 'pockets'.

5 Tack the wadding snowman shape to the back of the decorated felt snowman shape. With right sides together, match decorated wadding snowman shape to second felt shape leaving notched opening free. Back wadding with tissue paper – tear away after machining. Pin, tack and machine stitch with 1 cm (⅜ in) turnings using a small zig-zag stitch. Remove tacking. Trim seams down to 6 mm (¼ in). Carefully turn through to the right side, 'rolling out' felt shape to flatten. Pin and tack round edges of snowman to hold.

6 Pin and tack the trimmed wadding hat shape to one black felt hat shape. With felt shapes together, pin, tack and machine stitch with 6 mm (¼ in) turnings, using a small zig-zag stitch and leaving notched base open.

Trim turnings on curves. Remove tacking. Turn through to right side. Roll out seam with fingers. Tack to hold. On the right side of hat along base edge, catchstitch polyester wadding brim strip in position. Roll up hat to form brim and conceal wadding. Catchstitch at side seam. Catchstitch remaining robin to side of hat as photograph.

7 Place finished hat on snowman's head, wadding-backed felt to front. Pin and catchstitch to head at side seams.

8 Pin and tack the two carrot shapes together. Machine stitch with 3 mm (⅛ in) turnings. Turn through to right side. Using scraps of polyester wadding, stuff the carrot nose tightly. Position on face and catchstitch round base.

9 Sew on button eyes.

10 Join the 48 cm (19 in) × 6 cm (2½ in) scarf strips of scarlet felt on one short edge, taking a 6 mm (¼ in) seam. Fringe ends by cutting into each end for 7 cm (2¾ in) at 6 mm (¼ in) intervals.

11 Catchstitch each end of green ribbon at back of both shoulders and at 10 cm (4 in) intervals along back so that the ribbon is secured at the back of the head and in the middle of the hat.

12 Matching seam to centre back of snowman's neck, tie the scarf loosely around neck.

CHRISTMAS DOOR DECORATION

Welcome holiday guests to your home with this big, easy-to-make forest green wreath. Decorate it with tinsel, strings of Christmas beads, miniature crackers, fir cones and baubles of your choice and hang it on a front door that is protected from the elements for the whole of the festive season.

materials

florist's wire ring, 36 cm (14 in) outside diameter
1 m (39½ in) of 1 m (39½ in)-wide heavy weight polyester wadding
1 m (39½ in) of 1 m (39½ in)-wide lightweight polyester wadding
2 m (2¼ yd) of 115 cm (45 in)-wide forest green polyester lining fabric
various lengths of Christmas bead chains, tinsel, metallic ribbon or string
4 mini-crackers
mini-fruits on wire stems (from florist's)
scissors
matching thread (dark green)
2 pine cones, sprayed gold

to make

1 Cutting across the width of the polyester lining fabric and both waddings, cut as many 15 cm (6 in)-wide strips as possible. Set aside two strips of lining fabric to make the bow and loop for hanging.

2 To pad the wire ring, twist two of the heavy weight wadding strips to form a sausage shape and lay them inside the curve of the ring. Weave and bind the remaining heavyweight strips around them to pad out the ring. Catchstitch to secure.

Using lightweight wadding strips, bind the ring again to form a perfectly smooth shape. Catchstitch to secure.

3 Turn a 1 cm (⅜ in) hem on both long raw edges of all green fabric strips and lightly press to neaten. With pressed turnings to wadding ring, secure the end of one strip and lightly bind the padded circle. Catchstitch to hold. Covering the end of first strip with a new strip, continue binding until ring is completely covered. Turn under the raw edge on the last strip and catchstitch to secure.

4 Wind bead chains, tinsel and metallic ribbon or string around ring. Tuck crackers under tinsel and secure. Catchstitch mini-fruits to green lining fabric. Turn a 1 cm (⅜ in) hem on short sides of both remaining strips. Press in half lengthways. Use one strip to form a large loop for hanging. Knot firmly and catchstitch to ring to secure. Tie second fabric strip into a big floppy bow and catchstitch to ring to secure. Catchstitch pine cones on bottom of ring near bow.

RING VARIATIONS

The Christmas ring shown here could be made with a variety of different fabrics and then decorated accordingly. Try covering it with silver or gold lamé and then adorn it with pine cones sprayed in gold or silver. Alternatively wrap dress net around it in red and green, pinks and blues, or white. Spray crackers and seed heads in contrasting or matching colours. For a birthday cover the ring with flowers, ribbons, sweets and cookies instead.

APPLIQUÉ TABLECLOTH

This delicate white voile tablecloth and its six matching serviettes will enhance any holiday setting and is an especially attractive background for Christmas dinner itself. The edges are bound with a self-border and corners are decorated with white voile Christmas trees which are appliquéd and topstitched in position. This cloth is suitable for a rectangular table measuring 2 m (6 ft 6 in) × 90 cm (36 in).

materials

4.6 m (5 yd) of 150 cm (59 in)-wide white polyester/cotton voile
matching thread (white)
centimetre pattern paper
scissors, pencil

to make

1 Transfer the diagrams to centimetre pattern paper. Using these as your patterns, cut the following:
from polyester/cotton voile 240 cm (94½ in) × 150 cm (59 in) for tablecloth, 6 × 53 cm (20¾ in) squares, 7 large trees, 8 small trees.
2 Turn a 1 cm (⅜ in) hem twice on both long sides and then both short sides of tablecloth. Pin and tack to hold. Press. Keeping to wrong side and placing right sides together, fold a 5 cm (2 in) hem on each side and form a mitre by bringing the corners up together, creating a line from inner hem edges out to pointed corner. Pin, tack and machine stitch mitre seam with 1 cm (⅜ in) turnings. Remove tacking. Trim mitre seam down to 3 mm (⅛ in). Press seam open. Repeat for other corners. Carefully turn each mitred corner through to right side, pointing out corners to form a 5 cm (2 in) hem. Lightly steam press. Pin and tack along inner hem edge and folded edge to hold.
3 Set machine on an approximate stitch width just under 3 mm (⅛ in) satin stitch and work on the front of the tablecloth. Topstitch edges of hem to hold. Remove tacking and lightly steam press on the wrong side.

4 Working on the wrong side of the tablecloth, position three large and two small trees centrally, turning no hems. Pin and tack edges of trees to tablecloth. Position four large trees at corners as photograph. Pin and tack edges to hold. Using the 3 mm (⅛ in) satin stitch, carefully topstitch round the trees. Lightly steam press on tree side of cloth. Remove any visible tacking.
5 To make the serviettes, repeat hem edge as for the tablecloth, but turn a

7 cm (2¾ in) mitred hem.
6 Working on the wrong side of serviette, position one small tree to the left of centre so that the tree sits to the right on right side of serviette. Turning no hem, pin and tack. With 3 mm (⅛ in) satin stitch, topstitch carefully round tree shape. Remove tacking. Lightly steam press on tree side. Repeat for other serviettes.

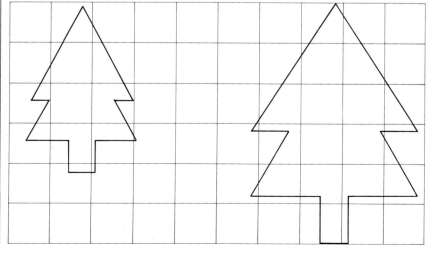

Scale   1 square = 5 cm (approx 2 in)

CHRISTMAS APRON

This practical and attractive bright red and green PVC apron will make the cook feel especially festive this Christmas. It has a decorative detachable band of berries, leaves and seed heads, and a roomy pocket. You could use the pattern given here to make a plain PVC apron for wearing the rest of the year, and leave off the velcro band and decorations at the top.

materials

70 cm (27½ in) of 122 cm (48 in)-wide berry print cotton-backed PVC
2 m (2¼ yd) of 2.5 cm (1 in)-wide woven cotton tape
24 cm (9½ in) of 2 cm (¾ in)-wide green velcro
matching thread (red)
scraps of green PVC
seed heads, imitation berries, fir cones
centimetre pattern paper
50 cm (20 in) of 3 mm (⅛ in) red or green ribbon
sellotape, ballpoint pen, teflon foot

to make

1 Transfer the diagrams to centimetre pattern paper. Using these as your patterns, cut the following:
from printed PVC 1 apron shape, 1 oblong 28 cm (11 in) × 19 cm (7½ in) for pocket, 1 decorative front band
from woven tape 3 × 66 cm (26 in) lengths (check head loop and side ties against your personal measurements)
from green PVC 6 leaf shapes.
2 Fold a 1.5 cm (⅝ in) turning across hem edge, hold with sellotape. Topstitch 1 cm (⅜ in) from edge. Position

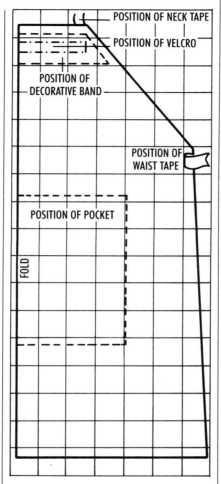

side tapes as diagram, hold with sellotape. Fold a 1.5 cm (⅝ in) turning, enclosing tape ends, and hold with sellotape. Topstitch sides 1 cm (⅜ in) from edge.
3 Position neck tape as diagram, hold with sellotape. Fold a 1.5 cm (⅝ in)

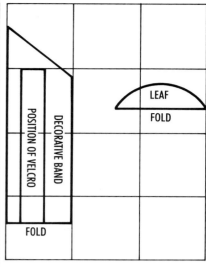

Scale   1 square = 5 cm (approx 2 in)

turning across top edge enclosing tape ends and hold with sellotape. Topstitch across neck edge. Remove all sellotape.
4 Fold a 1.5 cm (⅝ in) turning across top and bottom of pocket oblong, hold with sellotape. Topstitch close to edge. Repeat for both side edges. Remove sellotape. Position pocket as diagram. Hold with sellotape and topstitch along both sides and bottom 6 mm (¼ in) from edge, leaving top edge open. Remove sellotape.
5 Tear apart the 24 cm (9½ in) length of velcro. Position loop half centrally on right side across top of apron (as diagram). Tack and topstitch. Remove tacking. With wrong side of velcro to wrong side of PVC band, tack and topstitch. Remove tacking. Position PVC leaves, berries, seed heads and fir cones and tie ribbon as diagrams. Catchstitch to hold. Attach the decorative strip to the apron.

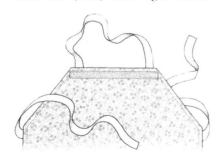

1 Tear velcro apart. Position it along the top of the apron, so it sits in the centre. Tack and topstitch to hold.

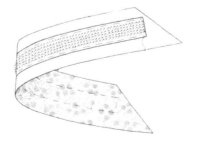

2 Place the wrong side of the other piece of velcro to the wrong side of the PVC band. Tack and topstitch.

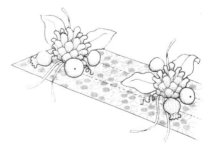

3 Arrange the leaves, berries, seed heads, fir cones and ribbon on the band and catchstitch to secure velcro to apron.

CHRISTMAS TABLE SET

This set of delightful, easy-to-make Christmas table decorations is made from printed cotton-backed PVC bound in brilliant red bias binding. The round mats and coasters are decorated with bright red berries, shiny green leaves, seed heads and fir cones. If you have some spare fabric, improvise and make a rectangular mat for the centre of the table.

materials for four sets

70 cm (27½ in) of 1.2 m (47 in)-wide berry print cotton-backed PVC
70 cm (27½ in) of 129 cm (51 in)-wide green kiss-laminated PVC (or 45 cm (17¾ in) of 150 cm (59 in)-wide cotton-backed PVC)
70 cm (27½ in) of 82 cm (32¼ in)-wide craft-quality vilene
9 m (10 yd) of 2.5 cm (1 in)-wide red cotton bias binding
2 m (2¼ yd) of 3 mm (⅛ in) red or green ribbon
1 m (1⅛ yd) of 2 cm (¾ in)-wide dark green velcro
various mini-fruits on stalks (from florist's)
4 pine cones
matching thread (red, green)
centimetre pattern paper
scissors, pencil, ballpoint pen

to make

1 Transfer the diagrams to centimetre pattern paper. Using these as your pattern, cut the following:

TABLEMATS

from cotton-backed PVC 4 mat circles, 4 mat crescent strips
from laminated PVC 4 mat circles, 24 leaves
from vilene 4 mat circles
from velcro 4 × 16 cm (6¼ in) lengths
from bias binding 4 × 108 cm (42½ in) lengths.

COASTERS

from cotton-backed PVC 4 coaster circles, 4 coaster crescent strips
from laminated PVC 4 coaster circles, 8 leaves
from vilene 4 coaster circles
from velcro 4 × 2 cm (¾ in) lengths
from bias binding 4 × 37 cm (14½ in) lengths.

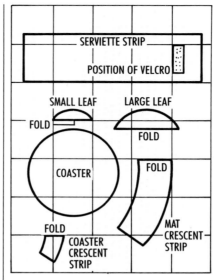

SERVIETTE STRIP
POSITION OF VELCRO
SMALL LEAF
LARGE LEAF
FOLD
FOLD
COASTER
FOLD
FOLD
COASTER CRESCENT STRIP
MAT CRESCENT STRIP

Scale 1 square = 5 cm (approx 2 in)

SERVIETTE RINGS

from cotton-backed PVC 4 serviette ring strips
from laminated PVC 4 serviette ring strips
from vilene 4 serviette ring strips
from velcro 4 × 4 cm (1½ in) lengths
from bias binding 8 × 25 cm (10 in) lengths, 8 × 7 cm (2¾ in lengths).

2 Tear a 16 cm (6¼ in) length of velcro in half and position wrong side of loop half to right side of one print PVC tablemat shape. Pin, tack and machine stitch, using red thread. Pin, tack and machine stitch hook half to wrong side of one large crescent strip. Repeat for other mats.

3 Tear a 2 cm (¾ in) length of velcro in half and position wrong side of loop

Scale 1 square = 5 cm (approx 2 in)

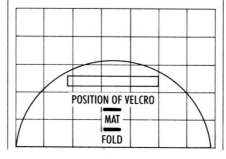

POSITION OF VELCRO
MAT
FOLD

half to right side of one print PVC coaster shape. Pin, tack and machine stitch. Pin, tack and machine stitch hook half to wrong side of a small crescent strip. Repeat for other coasters.

4 Tear a 4 cm (1½ in) length of velcro in half and position wrong side of loop half to right side of one printed PVC serviette ring (see photograph). Position wrong side of hook half on right side of plain PVC strip to correspond. Pin, tack and machine stitch. Repeat for other serviette rings.

5 Sandwich circles of vilene between wrong sides of corresponding circles of laminated and print PVC tablemats and coasters.

6 Sandwich strips of vilene between wrong sides of corresponding serviette ring strips of laminated and print PVC. Make sure velcro strips are at opposite ends of each ring.

7 Pin and tack 1.5 cm (⅝ in) from edges through three thicknesses on all mats, coasters and serviette rings.

8 Open out a 108 cm (42½ in) length of bias binding and place raw edge to curve of tacked triple-layer tablemat. Working on the crease and curving the binding as you go, pin, tack and machine stitch. Turn folded edge of binding to laminated side and catch-stitch. Repeat for all mats.

9 Repeat for coasters, using the 37 cm (14½ in) lengths of bias binding.

10 Open out 7 cm (2¾ in) lengths of binding and fold over raw edges on short ends of each serviette ring strip. Pin, tack and topstitch on folded edge.

11 Open out the 25 cm (10 in) lengths of binding and place raw edge to long sides of each strip. Pin, tack and topstitch on the folded edge, tucking in 1 cm (⅜ in) at each short end to neaten. Catchstitch to secure.

12 Fold each PVC leaf lengthways, make a tuck at base to form central vein, and topstitch down fold for spine. Position leaves spine down and arrange on strips. Catchstitch to strips at stem and oversew stalks of fruit in place. Use six leaves in pairs on each mat and two leaves on each coaster. Using ribbon, tie a pine cone around the centre set of leaves on each mat.

EASTER

After the dark gloomy winter months, Easter brings with it the first breath of spring. The gardens start to fill with flowers and there is a slight warmth in the air. Make some gifts to celebrate.

Announce the arrival of Easter at the breakfast table with a duck tea cosy and four duckling egg cosies. The yellow, cotton chintz duck on the tea cosy is padded out with polyester wadding, but as she is only attached to the blue tea cosy with velcro, she can be easily removed before washing. The smaller duck egg cosies are made from the same blue glazed cotton chintz as the tea cosy but the little chicks are depicted in yellow felt with scraps of orange felt for their beaks and feet.

Come up with some new tablemats, serviettes and serviette rings decorated with spring flowers for the holiday. Try to match the colour of the PVC backing with the floral cotton of the serviettes and finish the set off with bunches of fabric flowers in colours which echo those found in the material.

Eggs of the chocolate variety can be served up in Easter felt containers: a cheerful chick, an Easter bunny or a lamb. Fill them with tiny eggs and, if the weather is fine on Easter Sunday, hide them in the garden suspended from the branches of low trees and shrubs, and send the children off to look for them.

in this chapter

- Felt containers
- Easter table set
- Duck cosies

Right A table beautifully laid for breakfast on Easter Sunday with mats, serviettes and serviette rings all made from the same brightly coloured floral print, and pale blue and yellow duck tea cosy and duckling egg cosies, useful for keeping the tea and boiled eggs warm for later risers.

Left An Easter felt container, filled with tiny chocolate eggs for the children and padded out with shredded tissue paper.

FELT CONTAINERS

A bunny, a chick and a lamb carry lots of mini chocolate eggs for an Easter surprise. Decorate a spray of pussy-willow with these little containers holding a few tiny eggs, or make larger shapes using bigger circles of felt, to carry one large hollow egg!

You could adapt these designs to make party bags to hold going-home presents for a birthday party.

EASTER CHICK

materials

22 cm (8½ in) square of buttercup yellow felt
scraps of orange felt
50 cm (20 in) of 3 mm (⅛ in)-wide turquoise double satin ribbon
6 cm (2⅜ in) square of lightweight polyester wadding
small posy of fabric flowers
2 beads for eyes
matching thread (yellow)
bondaweb
centimetre pattern paper
scissors, pencil, thick card

to make

1 Transfer the diagrams to centimetre pattern paper and then to thick card. Using these as your patterns, cut the following:
from yellow felt 4 main body circles, 2 head circles, 2 wing shapes
from orange felt 1 beak shape, 2 foot shapes
from wadding 1 head circle
from bondaweb 2 body circles.

2 Fuse two yellow felt body circles together with one bondaweb circle, using a warm dry iron. Topstitch on extreme edge. Repeat with second pair of large yellow circles. Position orange felt feet on one stiffened felt circle as diagram. Pin and tack.

3 Sandwich wadding between the two felt head circles, sliding in orange felt beak. Pushing wadding in from edges, pin and tack head circles together. Position padded head on one stiffened body shape as photograph and slide wings under head circle as indicated. Pin and tack. Topstitch on extreme edge all around head circle.

4 Match the two stiffened body circles, wrong sides together. Pin, tack and topstitch round the bottom edge to halfway point, forming 'pocket' as on diagram.

5 Sew bead eyes on head circle (see photograph). Catchstitch posy of fabric flowers to centre top of head circle. Tie with a bow at one end of turquoise satin ribbon and loop remainder of ribbon over to back of stiffened body. Catchstitch ribbon back and front.

EASTER BUNNY

materials

22 cm (8½ in) square of silver grey felt
scraps of pink felt
50 cm (20 in) of 3 mm (⅛ in)-wide pink double satin ribbon
6 cm (2⅜ in) square of lightweight polyester wadding
1 cm (⅜ in) pink acrylic pom-pon
2 cm (¾ in) white acrylic pom-pon
matching thread (grey)
small pink fabric flowers
2 beads for eyes
bondaweb
scrap of craft-quality vilene or white felt for front teeth
centimetre pattern paper, thick card
scissors, pencil

to make

1 Transfer the diagrams to centimetre pattern paper and then to thick card. Using these as your patterns, cut the following:
from grey felt 4 body circles, 2 head circles, 2 outer ear shapes, 2 paw shapes
from pink felt 2 inner ear shapes
from bondaweb 2 body circles
from wadding 1 × 5.5 cm (2¼ in) head circle
from scrap of vilene pair of front teeth.

2 Fuse two grey felt body circles together with one bondaweb circle. Topstitch on extreme edge. Repeat for second pair of grey circles. Position and tack the grey felt paws to one stiffened felt circle as in photograph.

3 Place pink and grey ear pieces together, turning base of double ear inwards to form fold. Pin and tack them to one of the small grey felt head circles.

4 Sandwich wadding head circle between the two grey felt circles, placing tacked ears to wadding side. Slide vilene front teeth between the circles on the opposite side to ears. Pin and tack head circles together. Position padded head on one stiffened body shape as diagram. Pin and tack. Topstitch on extreme edge of head circle. Remove tacking.

5 Place the two stiffened body circles wrong sides together. Pin, tack and topstitch round the bottom edge to halfway point, forming 'pocket'.

6 Sew on bead eyes and pink pom-pon nose. Catchstitch fabric flowers between ears. Tie a bow at one end of pink satin ribbon and loop remainder of ribbon to back for hanging. Catchstitch front and back to hold. Catchstitch white pom-pon tail to centre of stiffened back body.

EASTER LAMB

materials

22 cm (8½ in) square of white felt
scraps of black felt
50 cm (20 in) of 3 mm (⅜ in)-wide white double satin ribbon
12 cm (4¾ in) × 7 cm (2¾ in) lightweight polyester wadding
1 thin black pipecleaner
1 cm (⅜ in) black acrylic pom-pon
2 cm (¾ in) white acrylic pom-pon
small posy of fabric flowers
2 beads for eyes
matching thread (white)
bondaweb
centimetre pattern paper
scissors, pencil, thick card, iron

to make

1 Transfer the diagrams to centimetre pattern paper and then to the thick card. Using these as your patterns, cut the following:

from white felt 4 main body circles, 1 head circle

from black felt 2 ear shapes

from bondaweb 2 × 11cm (4¼in) body circles

from wadding 1 woolly crescent, 1 fringe triangle with 1.5cm (⅝in) sides.

2 Fuse two white felt body circles together with one bondaweb circle. Topstitch on extreme edge. Repeat for second pair of white body circles. Cut the black pipecleaner in half, bend each half in half again. Catchstitch to wrong side of one stiffened white body circle.

3 Join stiffened body circles to halfway mark as diagram. Pin, tack and topstitch round bottom, forming 'pocket' edge, avoiding the pipecleaner feet with the machine needle.

4 Place wadding half circle at top of front stiffened body circle as diagram. Pin and catchstitch.

5 Position pom-pon nose, bead eyes, felt ears and wadding hair fringe triangle. Catchstitch to head circle as photograph. Catchstitch top of head circle to wadding half circle.

6 Catchstitch posy. Tie a bow at one end of white ribbon and loop remainder of ribbon to back to form hanger loop. Catchstitch ribbon front and back.

7 Catchstitch white pom-pon tail on centre of back body.

FACIAL FEATURES

Ready-to-buy plastic eyes, noses and ears are all available, but it's cheaper and more fun to improvise. Use buttons or pom-pons for noses and tiny beads or star-shaped sequins for the eyes.

Felt can be cut into suitable shapes to represent these features as well, and also makes a good mouth or set of whiskers. For hair, a beard or moustache, cut out some polyester wadding.

Scale 1 square = 5cm (approx 2in)

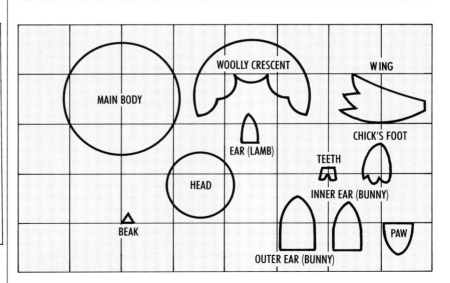

MAIN BODY

WOOLLY CRESCENT

WING

EAR (LAMB)

CHICK'S FOOT

TEETH

HEAD

INNER EAR (BUNNY)

BEAK

OUTER EAR (BUNNY)

PAW

EASTER TABLE SET

Bring a breath of springtime into the house with the pretty bright colours of fresh spring flowers. The place mats and serviette rings are made from printed cotton-backed PVC, lined with a plain kiss-laminated PVC and decorated with pretty fabric flowers in coordinating colours. The serviettes are simple hemmed squares made from easy-to-launder cotton polyester in a print that matches the printed PVC.

materials to make 3 place settings

40 cm (15¾ in) of 140 cm (55 in)-wide printed cotton-backed PVC
50 cm (20 in) of 140 cm (55 in)-wide matching or toning polyester/cotton print
70 cm (27½ in) of 129 cm (51 in)-wide lime green kiss-laminated PVC
80 cm (31½ in) of 82 cm (32¼ in)-wide craft-quality vilene
7 m (7⅔ yds) of 2.5 cm (1 in)-wide yellow cotton bias binding
13.5 cm (5¼ in) of 2 cm (¾ in)-wide velcro
1.5 m (59 in) of 1 cm (⅜ in)-wide red double satin ribbon
bunches of fabric spring flowers
matching thread (white, yellow)
scissors, ruler, pencil, ballpoint pen, teflon foot

to make

1 Cut the following:
from printed cotton-backed PVC (on wrong side, marking with pencil) 3 place mat oblongs, each 45 cm (17¾ in) × 33 cm (13 in), 3 serviette rings, each 23 cm (9 in) × 7 cm (2¾ in)
from polyester/cotton print 3 × 50 cm (20 in) serviette squares
from laminated PVC (on wrong side, marking with pen) 3 place mat oblongs, each 45 cm (17¾ in) × 33 cm (13 in), 3 serviette rings, each 23 cm (9 in) × 7 cm (2¾ in)
from vilene 3 place mat oblongs, each 45 cm (17¾ in) × 33 cm (13 in), 3 serviette rings 23 cm (9 in) × 7 cm (2¾ in)
from bias binding 6 × 47 cm (18½ in) lengths, 6 × 35 cm (13¾ in) lengths
from velcro 3 × 4.5 cm (1¾ in) lengths
from ribbon 3 × 50 cm (20 in) lengths.
2 Tear apart one 4.5 cm (1¾ in) length of velcro and position hook piece as diagram, wrong side to the right side of printed PVC serviette ring. Position

loop half of velcro on shiny side of laminated PVC. Pin, tack and machine stitch the velcro to both sides of the serviette ring. Repeat for the other rings.

3 Position centre of one 50 cm (20 in) length of ribbon approximately 10 cm (4 in) in from top left hand corner of printed PVC mat, diagonally. Pin, tack and machine stitch across width of ribbon to hold.
4 Sandwich oblongs of vilene between corresponding wrong sides of lamin-

ated PVC and printed PVC for mats. Pin and tack approximately 6 mm (¼ in) from the edges through all three thicknesses. Repeat for all the other mats.

5 Sandwich serviette ring oblongs of vilene between wrong sides of printed PVC and laminated PVC, with velcro pieces at opposite ends of the strips. Pin, tack and topstitch approximately 6 mm (¼ in) from edges through all three thicknesses. Repeat for other strips. Join velcro to form a ring. Decorate centre fronts with two fabric flowers. Catchstitch to secure the flowers.

6 Open out one 35 cm (13¾ in) length of bias binding. Place right side raw edges to one short side of tacked mat. Pin, tack and machine stitch on the 1.2 cm (½ in) crease. Remove tacking. Turn folded edge of bias to laminated side and catchstitch. Repeat for the other short side and for all of the place mats.

Open out one 47 cm (18½ in) length of bias binding. Place right side and raw edges to one long side of tacked mat, turning under 1 cm (⅜ in) at each end of binding to neaten. Pin, tack and machine stitch on the 1.2 cm (½ in) crease. Remove tacking. Turn folded edge of bias binding to laminated side of mat and catchstitch. Repeat for other side and for all mats. Decorate front with a bunch of spring flowers secured with thread and tied to mat with ribbon. Tie a bow and cut the ends of ribbon at a slant to finish.

7 Turn a 1 cm (⅜ in) hem to wrong side on all four edges of serviette square. Pin, tack and machine stitch. Remove tacking. Press.

Keeping to wrong side and placing right sides together, fold a 5 cm (2 in) hem on each side and form a mitre by bringing the corners up together, creating a line from inner hem edges out to pointed corner. Pin, tack and machine stitch mitre seam with 1 cm (⅜ in) turnings. Remove tacking. Trim mitre seam down to 3 mm (⅛ in). Press seam open. Repeat for other corners. Carefully turn each mitred corner through to right side, pointing out corners to form a 5 cm (2 in) hem.

Lightly steam press. Pin and tack along inner hem edge and folded edge to hold. Topstitch, working from wrong side, 3 mm (⅛ in) from inner hem edge. Remove tacking. Repeat for other serviettes.

TEFLON FOOT AND NEEDLE

If you are working with PVC a lot, it pays to buy a teflon foot and needle for your sewing machine. Covered in black teflon, the foot prevents the PVC from sticking on the metal teeth or feed dogs. The needle, also covered in black teflon, pierces the plastic-coated cotton with great precision.

DUCK COSIES

A cheeky bow-tied duck with her charming family of ducklings will brighten up your Easter breakfast table. The blue cotton chintz cosies are decorated with yellow birds.

TEA COSY

materials

- 35 cm (13¾ in) of 140 cm (55 in)-wide blue glazed cotton chintz
- 35 cm (13¾ in) of 140 cm (55 in)-wide yellow glazed cotton chintz
- 30 cm (11¾ in) of 1 m (39½ in)-wide medium weight polyester wadding
- 30 cm (11¾ in) of 1 m (39½ in)-wide light-weight polyester wadding
- 2 pieces 12 cm (4¾ in) × 6 cm (2⅜ in) of red and white spotted cotton
- 54 cm (21¼ in) of 2 cm (¾ in)-wide sky blue velcro
- bondaweb
- 1 large blue bead for eye
- matching thread (yellow, sky blue, red)
- centimetre pattern paper
- scissors, pencil

to make

1 Transfer the diagrams to centimetre pattern paper, and cut the following:
from blue chintz 4 tea cosy shapes, 1 oblong 11 cm (4¼ in) × 6.5 cm (2½ in) for loop
from yellow chintz 1 left and 1 right duck shape, 1 left and 1 right wing shape
from velcro 2 × 20 cm (8 in) lengths, 2 × 7 cm (2¾ in) lengths
from medium weight wadding 2 cosy shapes
from lightweight wadding 1 duck, 1 wing.

2 With right sides together, join two blue chintz cosy shapes to form the lining. Pin, tack and machine stitch. Remove tacking. On the long straight base edge, turn up a 6 mm (¼ in) hem to wrong side. Pin, tack and machine stitch on curved seam. Press edge.

3 Tear apart the two 20 cm (8 in) velcro lengths. Position both hook pieces centrally to right sides of cosy lining, parallel to turned hem edge. Pin, tack and machine stitch. Remove tacking. Turn a further 2.5 cm (1 in) hem to wrong side on cosy lining. Pin, tack and machine stitch. Remove tacking.

4 With right sides together, fold blue chintz oblong in half lengthways. Pin, tack and machine stitch long edge. Remove tacking. Turn through to right side. Press seam to centre.

5 Position 7 cm (2¾ in) velcro hook strips on 1 cosy piece as diagram. Pin, tack and machine stitch. Remove tacking. Place wadding cosy pieces to wrong sides of cosy pieces. Pin and tack. Fold stitched chintz loop oblong in half and match raw edges. Position at centre top of one cosy shape so that folded end of loop hangs down on to right side of cosy. Pin, then tack. With right sides of chintz main cosy pieces together, pin and tack to hold. Machine stitch using a small zig-zag stitch and taking 1 cm (⅜ in) turnings.

6 Turn a 6 mm (¼ in) hem to wrong side on long straight edge of cosy. Pin, tack and machine stitch. Position the two 20 cm (8 in) lengths of velcro loops inside main cosy piece to correspond to the lining. Pin, tack and machine stitch parallel to bottom of main cosy. Remove tacking. Turn up a further 2.5 cm (1 in) hem on to wadding. Pin, tack and catchstitch. Remove tacking. Turn through to right side.

7 Place the wadding wing to the wrong side of chintz top wing. Pin and tack. With right sides of one left and one right wing shape together, pin, tack and machine stitch, beginning and ending at notched opening and taking 3 mm (⅛ in) turnings. Remove tacking. Turn through to right side. Slide turnings on opening to inside, pin and catchstitch. Press lightly. Tack round shape of wing to hold. Topstitch feather markings.

8 Position 7 cm (2¾ in) velcro loop strips on right-facing (bottom) duck piece. Pin, tack and machine stitch. Remove tacking. Place wadding duck on wrong side of left-facing duck (top duck). Pin and tack. Position wing as photograph. Pin and tack. Topstitch 3 mm (⅛ in) from edge as diagram. Remove tacking.

9 With right sides of duck shapes together and tucking wing tip away from machine, pin, tack and machine stitch, beginning and ending at notched opening and taking 6 mm (¼ in) turnings. Remove tacking. Turn through, pushing out beak and tail and snipping into any corners. Slide turnings on opening to inside. Pin, tack and catchstitch to close.

10 Using a warm dry iron, fuse bondaweb to one 12 cm (4¾ in) × 6 cm (2⅜ in) spotted oblong. Place bow tie pattern on paper side of bondaweb. Draw outline and cut out shape. Peel off paper. Iron on to wrong side of a second spotted oblong. Cut original bow shape again. Place stiffened bow tie across the neck of duck. Pin and tack across centre of bow shape to hold. Topstitch top and bottom edges. Remove tackings. Sew on bead eye.

11 Join the duck to cosy by velcro.

EGG COSIES

materials for 4 egg cosies

- 50 cm (20 in) × 35 cm (13¾ in) blue glazed cotton
- 50 cm (20 in) × 35 cm (13¾ in) cotton print fabric
- 2 × 22 cm (8½ in) squares of yellow felt
- scraps of orange felt
- 50 cm (20 in) × 35 cm (13¾ in) polyester wadding
- 2 × 22 cm (8 in) squares of bondaweb
- 8 small beads
- matching thread (blue)
- centimetre pattern paper, scissors

to make

1 Transfer diagrams to centimetre pattern paper. Cut 8 cosy shapes from the cotton, print fabric and wadding.

2 Using a warm dry iron, fuse bondaweb to yellow and orange felt. Cut a yellow head and body and an orange beak and feet for each cosy.

3 Peel paper backing from bondaweb and position feet at base of one cosy shape. Position body, beak and head in that order. Sew on beads for eyes.

4 Place wrong side of cotton print cosy lining to wadding and tack. With right sides of two cotton print lining shapes together, take 6 mm (¼ in) turnings and machine stitch round cosy shapes.

5 With right sides together, pin and tack two blue cosy pieces (one decorated, one plain). With 6 mm (¼ in) turnings, machine stitch together. Turn through to right side. Slide padded lining into turned cosy. Turning a 6 mm (¼ in) hem, pin and catchstitch.

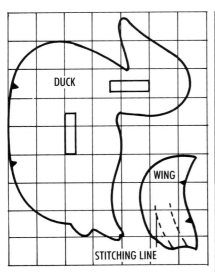

DUCK

WING

STITCHING LINE

Scale 1 square = 5 cm (approx 2 in)

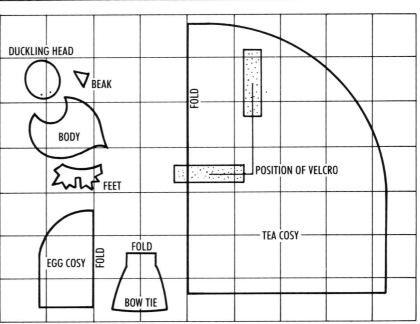

DUCKLING HEAD

BEAK

BODY

FEET

FOLD

POSITION OF VELCRO

TEA COSY

EGG COSY

FOLD

FOLD

BOW TIE

HALLOWE'EN AND THANKSGIVING

In the lull between summer and Christmas, make gifts for Thanksgiving and Hallowe'en.

A harvest garland to hang on the door, for harvest festivals or Thanksgiving, provides you with the opportunity to make use of all dried flowerheads, nuts and pine cones collected on country walks. There are numerous ways to decorate it. Follow the designs here or come up with your own decorations, once you have made the basic ring. When Hallowe'en arrives at the end of October, let your imagination run wild. Create weird and wonderful objects with black, grey and murky green fabrics. Slippers decorated with a gruesome spider made from black pipe-cleaners, an ugly felt frog, or a witch's face would all be great fun to wear at a fancy dress party.

To keep young children amused on the day, put together a pair of witch puppets. Wearing black cloaks, typical witch's hats and, or course, each carrying a broom stick, they can be used in the rainbow puppet theatre on page 14.

At teatime, mark the occasion with a cake frill stitched together from black and white gingham and crawling with spiders, like those made for the spider slipper. If you make masses of these pipe-cleaner spiders you can suspend them on thin red ribbons attached to a black padded ring, to make a creepy mobile.

in this chapter

Right These four children have started preparing for the Hallowe'en party before all their friends arrive. They have decorated a cake with the black-and-white gingham cake frill, put on the Hallowe'en slippers (to complement their face masks) and made a spooky spider mobile and two witch puppets. Notice the Thanksgiving garland hanging on the cupboard at the back of the kitchen, ready for celebrations in November.
Left A pair of witch puppets on sticks, with wonderful witchy clothes.

THANKSGIVING GARLAND

Bring the russet and golds of autumn to your home and extend a front porch welcome at thanksgiving or harvest festival time. You can collect the teasels, poppy heads, hazelnut cases and fir cones on a country walk, or town dwellers can find a good selection of seed heads as many florist's shops. Use them to decorate this softly-padded ring which will remind family and friends of harvest bounty.

materials

florist's wire ring, outside diameter 36 cm (14 in)
75 cm (29½ in) of heavy weight polyester wadding
40 cm (15¾ in) of lightweight polyester wadding
1 m (39½ in) of 115 cm (45 in)-wide brown polyester dress lining fabric
5 × 30 cm (11¾ in) lengths of 115 cm (45 in)-wide polyester dress lining fabrics in contrasting shades of rust and gold
1 reel florist's wire
selection of dried seed heads, fir cones, etc
matching threads (brown, rust, gold)
scissors, wire cutters

to make

1 Cut the lining fabrics and the waddings into strips 15 cm (6 in)-wide, using all the fabric and wadding. Cut across the width of the fabric so finished strips will be 115 cm (45 in) long.

2 Twist two of the heavy weight wadding strips to form a 'sausage' shape and place inside the curve of the wire ring. Wind remaining heavy weight wadding strips around frame to pad it out. Catchstitch to hold. Wrap the padded ring shape firmly with the lightweight wadding strips to give a perfectly smooth shape. Catchstitch to hold.

3 Using the basic brown lining, cover the padded ring completely. Catchstitch to hold.

4 Wrap the florist's wire once around ring and secure with a small twist. Continue to wind wire loosely around the ring, leaving gaps of 8 cm (3 in). Secure with a twist and trim with wire cutters.

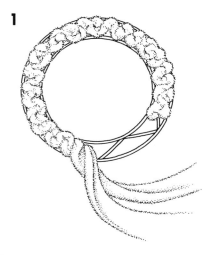

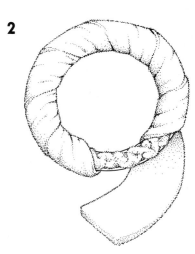

1 Take two of the 115 cm (45½ in)-long heavy weight wadding strips and twist them to form a bulky sausage-like shape. Place these heavy weight wadding strips inside the curve of the florist's wire ring to pad it out well.

2 Wind the other heavy weight wadding strips all around the outside of the florist's ring, covering it completely, then catchstitch. Wrap the lightweight wadding strips firmly and tightly around the ring, covering the heavy weight wadding, to achieve a smooth finish. Catchstitch to hold.

3 Take the strips of brown lining fabric, and wrap them around the ring in a similar motion to the wadding strips, until the ring is completely covered and no wadding is showing. Neatly catchstitch the brown lining strips to hold them in position and give a neat, finished look.

4 Wrap florist's wire around the padded ring, once and secure. Then wrap it around again more loosely and secure with a twist. Tuck dried seed heads, fir cones, etc under the wire and hold them in place with a few stitches. Tie the lengths of remaining lining in bows to help cover the wire and decorate.

5 Tuck seed heads, fir cones, etc under wire, arranging them attractively, and anchor with a few stitches. Decorate the ring with the remaining lengths of contrasting linings, tied roughly into bows and knots to cover any visible wire. Press one length of the contrast lining in half lengthways and form a huge loop, knotted once, for hanging.

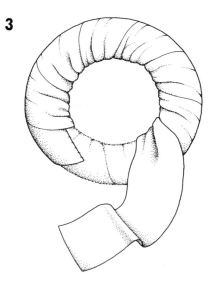

These padded mule slippers are decorated to frighten off Hallowe'en tricksters. The basic pattern is given for the largest size and can be reduced by cutting, overlapping and decreasing shapes to fit any size foot. And the decorations can be adapted to suit other occasions.

BASIC SLIPPER PATTERN

materials for 1 pair

60 cm (23½ in) square of wide main fabric
25 cm (10 in) of 1 m (39½ in)-wide lightweight polyester wadding
25 cm (10 in) of 82 cm (32¼ in)-wide craft-quality vilene
matching thread
centimetre pattern paper
sheet of thin card large enough for whole personal pattern
scissors, ruler, pencil, tailor's chalk, sellotape

to make

1 Transfer the diagrams to centimetre pattern paper. Stand with one bare foot on the inner sole piece A and draw around your own foot within this shape. Measure your traced shape and compare it with the pattern given. Allowing 1 cm (⅜ in) turnings around the slipper, alter the size by cutting the broken lines and overlapping vertically and horizontally. Sellotape pattern and reshape front slipper (B) to match inner sole (A). Redraw all pattern pieces on thin card and cut the following:
from main fabric 2 inner soles turned at fold (piece A), 4 front slippers turned at fold (piece B), 2 front bottom soles turned at fold (piece C), 2 back bottom soles turned at fold (piece D)
from polyester wadding 2 inner soles turned at fold (A), 2 front slippers turned at fold (B)
from vilene 2 inner soles turned at fold (A).
2 To join main fabric front slipper pieces (B), place right sides together with one wadding shape to one wrong side. Pin to hold. Pin, tack and machine stitch with 6 mm (¼ in) turnings across

the vamp edge of front slipper pieces (dotted line). Remove tacking. Trim turnings to 3 mm (⅛ in) and snip into curved shape. Turn to right side. Pin and tack shapes around complete slipper front to hold. Repeat for other slipper.
3 On the straight edges of front and back main fabric bottom sole pieces (C and D), turn a 1 cm (⅜ in) hem to wrong side to neaten. Pin, tack and machine stitch. Press. Repeat for other slipper.
4 Pin and tack the wadding to the wrong side of the inner sole (A). Pin and tack the vilene to the wadding. Repeat for other slipper.
5 With padded side uppermost, lay the

slipper fronts (B) on the right side of the padded inner soles (A). Pin and tack. Repeat for other slipper.
6 Lay the right side of the neatened front bottom sole (C) on the right side of padded front (B). Lay right side of back bottom sole (D) on turned hem (C) and right side of inner sole (A).

Working through all the thicknesses, pin, tack and machine stitch, taking 1 cm (⅜ in) turnings. Remove tacking and trim 6 mm (¼ in) from turnings. Trim vilene close to stitching line. Repeat for other slipper.
7 Open the bottom sole (C & D) pieces and pull the slipper shape through. Roll out edges of padded slipper shape to flatten. Pin and catch-stitch the neatened edge of front slipper (C) to back slipper (D). Repeat for other slipper.

 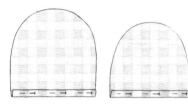

1 Join the front slipper pieces, placing the right sides of the fabric together and placing one wadding shape to one wrong side. Pin to hold in position. Then tack and stitch along the vamp edge only. Turn to right side.

2 Neaten the straight edges of both bottom sole pieces, by turning a 1 cm (⅜ in) hem to the wrong side of the fabric. Pin, tack and then machine stitch along the hem you've just turned and then press well.

 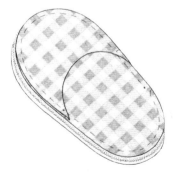

3 Place the wadding pieces to the wrong side of the inner sole and pin and tack. Next pin and tack the craft-quality vilene pieces to the wadding you have just attached to the slipper's inner sole.

4 Place the slipper fronts (from step 1), with the padded side showing uppermost, on the right side of the slipper's padded inner soles, stitched together in step 3. Pin and tack them in position.

Scale 1 square = 5 cm (approx 2 in)

TO DECORATE SLIPPERS

FROG

materials

60 cm (23½ in) square of olive green felt
60 cm (23½ in) square of lime green felt
scraps of leaf green, dark green and yellow felt
60 cm (23½ in) square of lightweight polyester wadding
4 × 7 mm (³⁄₈ in)-diameter joggle eyes
matching thread (light green, yellow, dark green)
centimetre pattern paper, card
fabric adhesive, scissors, pencil, ruler

to make

1 Make the basic slippers from olive green felt.
2 Transfer the diagrams to centimetre pattern paper and then to card. Using these as your patterns, cut the following:
from lime green felt 4 frogs, 2 eyelids
from leaf green felt 2 half lily pads (one for

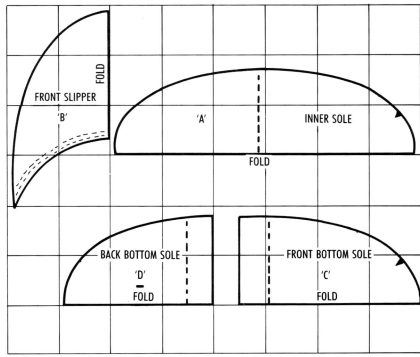

each slipper)
from dark green felt 12 small triangles
from yellow felt 4 × 5 cm (2 in)-diameter circles
from wadding 2 frog shapes.
3 Position each half lily pad on the outside front of each slipper. Pin and

catchstitch. Fold yellow circles in four and snip halfway in to form fringed edges. Gather centres and position two on each half lily pad. Catchstitch.
4 Sandwich one wadding shape between two felt frog shapes. Pin and tack. Topstitch 3 mm (⅛ in) from edges all

around each frog. Remove tacking. Position eyelids. Catchstitch rounded edges to hold. Using fabric adhesive, glue joggle eyes under lids and six dark green felt triangles to frog back. Repeat for other slipper.

5 Catchstitch frog shapes to slipper fronts along straight edges of lily pads.

SPIDER

materials

60 cm (23½ in) square of black-and-white gingham
2 × 4 cm (1½ in)-diameter black acrylic pom-pons
8 × 1.2 cm (½ in) black chenille pipe cleaners
matching thread (black)
4 joggle eyes, 2 cm (¾ in) in diameter
fabric adhesive

to make

1 Make the basic slippers from black-and-white gingham fabric. To make the spiders, form a star shape by criss-crossing the four pipecleaners, intertwining at centre to hold firm. Pin and tack to acrylic pom-pon. Carefully catch-stitch to secure. Bend pipecleaner at halfway point to form 'knees' and bend approximately 1.5 cm (⅝ in) from ends to form feet. Using fabric adhesive, glue joggle eyes to pom-pon. Repeat for other spider. Catchstitch bottom of acrylic body of spiders to slippers to secure.

WITCHES

materials

60 cm (23½ in) square of black polyester/cotton fabric
2 × 7 cm (2¾ in)-diameter polystyrene balls
2 × 31 cm (12 in) squares of green nylon stocking fabric
2 × 31 cm (12 in) squares of black nylon stocking fabric
2 × 22 cm (8½ in) squares of black felt
2 × 30 cm (11¾ in) squares of lightweight polyester wadding
bondaweb
4 tiny coloured star sequins

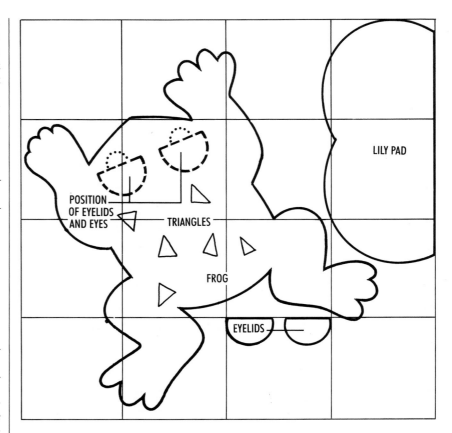

LILY PAD

POSITION OF EYELIDS AND EYES

TRIANGLES

FROG

EYELIDS

Scale   1 square = 5 cm (approx 2 in)

2 imitation mini-limes on wire stalks (from florist's)
2 large mauve sequins, 1 cm (⅜ in) in diameter,
2 red beads
matching thread (black)
centimetre pattern paper
non-spirit base fabric adhesive, ballpoint pen, ruler, scissors

to make

1 Make the basic slippers using black polyester/cotton fabric.

2 Transfer the diagrams on page 134 to centimetre pattern paper. Using these as your patterns, cut the following:
from black felt 2 hat crowns, 4 hat brim rings, 4 eye outlines
from bondaweb 2 hat brim circles.

3 Secure the centre of one 30 cm (11¾ in) square of wadding to the top of the ball head with a pin. Pull the wadding down to make the neck. Secure by binding with thread. Cover with the square of green stocking fabric and bind with thread as before.

4 Fold one square of black stocking fabric in three. Snip along two thirds of square at 6 mm (¼ in) intervals to form strands of long stringy hair. Unfold. Gather uncut end of square and catchstitch to crown of head.

5 Using a warm, dry iron, fuse the two brim shapes together with bondaweb circles.

6 Form a cone shape with a felt crown triangle, overlap at centre back and catchstitch seam together. Place crown on head. Pin and catchstitch to stocking fabric and wadding. Drop stiffened brim over hat and position on edge of hat. Pin and catchstitch it to secure in position.

7 Using non-spirit base adhesive, decorate face as photograph, placing two black felt eye outlines and small stars for eyes. Press stalk of mini-lime into polystyrene head for nose. Position the large round sequin centrally for the mouth. Sew on with a red bead to secure in position. Repeat for the second witch head.

8 Catchstitch the witches to the slipper fronts by the necks and tie the loose strands of hair to cover the raw edge of neck.

SPIDER MOBILE

Creepy crawlies hang from a sinister black ring to add a touch of fright to a Hallowe'en party. The spiders are quickly made from black acrylic pompons, in two different sizes, and pipecleaners and attached with ribbon.

Hang the mobile over the party table and watch the guests, young and old, as they react to the web of spiders that has joined the party.

materials

10 × 3 cm (1¼ in)-diameter black acrylic pom-pons
10 × 2 cm (¾ in)-diameter black acrylic pom-pons
60 thin black pipecleaners 17 cm (6½ in) long
10 m (11 yd) of 3 mm (⅛ in)-wide red double satin ribbon
60 cm (23½ in) square of black felt
30 cm (11¾ in) of 1 m (39½ in)-wide light-weight polyester wadding
matching thread (black)
1 wooden embroidery hoop, 13 cm (5 in) in diameter
scissors, ballpoint pen, ruler

to make

1 Cut the following:
from black felt 6 strips each 60 cm (23½ in) × 4 cm (1½ in)
from red ribbon 20 lengths, varying from 50 cm (20 in) to 30 cm (11¾ in), 2 × 80 cm (31½ in) lengths for hanging
from wadding 5 strips, each 1 m (39½ in) × 6 cm (2⅜ in)
from pipe cleaners cut 20 pipecleaners in half (legs for small spiders).
2 Using the wadding, bind the inner ring of the embroidery hoop. Pin and catchstitch the beginning of each wadding strip as you work. Bind the wadding ring with the strips of black felt. Catchstitch as you bind.
3 To make a large spider, form a star shape by criss-crossing four whole pipecleaners, turning once at the centre to intertwine them. Oversew centre to hold. Catchstitch each set of eight legs to a large pom-pon. Bend pipecleaners at halfway point to form 'knees' and approximately 1 cm (⅜ in) from ends to form 'feet'. Repeat to make 10 large spiders.

4 To make small spiders, make as large spider, using halves of pipecleaners and small acrylic pom-pons.
5 Make a small bow on one end of each red ribbon length. Pin and catchstitch a bow to the top of each spider. Tie the other ends around padded ring.
6 To make the hanger, make a small bow at each end of the 80 cm (31½ in) lengths of ribbon. Tie each end to opposite sides of the padded ring carefully, placing the bows on top of the ring. Catchstitch to hold. Catchstitch bows of spiders' ribbons to hold, when mobile is balanced.

BALANCING A MOBILE

It is essential that a mobile has good balance if it is to look attractive. Once the hanging objects are assembled, it may be necessary to juggle them around slightly to keep the padded ring level. Therefore, never secure the looped ribbons holding the objects on to the padded ring until you have achieved a perfect balance. Using two crossed lengths of ribbon instead of one to suspend the mobile padded ring should also help to keep it level.

HALLOWE'EN DECORATIONS

The goblins will play on Hallowe'en, and the house will seem covered with creepy-crawlies! The witches can stage their own puppet show or go along for a trick or two. The cake frill can be altered to fit a cake of any size.

WITCH PUPPETS

materials for 2 witches

2 × 7 cm (2¾ in)-diameter polystyrene balls
2 × 25 cm (10 in) lengths of 6 mm (¼ in)-diameter wooden dowelling
2 × 34 cm (13¼ in) lengths of 1 cm (⅜ in)-square wooden rod
2 × 31 cm (12 in) squares of green nylon stocking fabric
2 × 31 cm (12 in) squares of black nylon stocking fabric
2 × 60 cm (23½ in) squares of silver grey felt
2 × 60 cm (23½ in) squares of black felt
2 × 22 cm (8½ in) squares of brown felt
2 × 30 cm (11¾ in) square of lightweight polyester wadding
bondaweb
4 tiny coloured star sequins
2 imitation mini-fruit limes on wire stalks (from florist's)
2 large mauve sequins, 1 cm (⅜ in) in diameter
2 jumbo chenille pipecleaners, 1.2 cm (½ in)-diameter in serpent green
2 miniature chenille frogs (from florist's)
matching thread (white, grey, black)
centimetre pattern paper
spirit and non-spirit base fabric adhesives, ballpoint pen, ruler, sharp-pointed scissors, craft knife

to make each witch

1 Transfer the diagrams to centimetre pattern paper. Using these as your patterns, cut the following:
from silver grey felt 1 dress, 1 oblong 25 cm (10 in) × 5 cm (2 in) for stick
from black felt 1 cloak, 1 hat crown, 2 eye outlines, 2 hat brim rings, 1 oblong 25 cm (10 in) × 3.5 cm (1⅜ in) for broomsticks
from brown felt 1 oblong 25 cm (10 in) × 9 cm (3½ in) for broom head
from bondaweb 1 hat brim.
2 Apply a coat of spirit base adhesive to 25 cm (10 in) of the square wooden rod. Repeat for whole length of wooden dowelling, black felt broomstick oblong and grey felt oblong. When tacky, place rod on adhesive side of grey felt and turn slowly to cover rod, smoothing all the time. Repeat with black felt for dowelling.
3 Using sharp pointed scissors or a craft knife, carve a 1 cm (⅜ in) square out of the polystyrene ball. Fill hole with non-spirit base fabric adhesive and slide in wooden (uncovered) end of square wooden rod. Allow to set.
4 Secure the centre of one 30 cm (11¾ in) square of wadding to the top of the ball head with a pin. Pull the wadding down to neck and secure by binding with thread. Leave frill of wadding to form shoulders. Tie knot to hold. Cover with green stocking fabric and secure in the same way.
5 To make the witch's dress and cloak, wrap grey felt dress round wadding shoulders, overlapping centre back slightly. Pin and catchstitch seam together. Repeat for black cloak, fastening at front.
6 Fold one black stocking fabric square in three and snip upwards two thirds of the way into square at intervals of 6 mm (¼ in) to make long stringy hair. Unfold. Gather uncut end of square and catchstitch to crown of head.
7 Using a warm, dry iron, fuse together the two brim shapes with bondaweb.
    Form a cone shape with hat crown triangle, overlap at centre back and

Scale 1 square = 5 cm (approx 2 in)

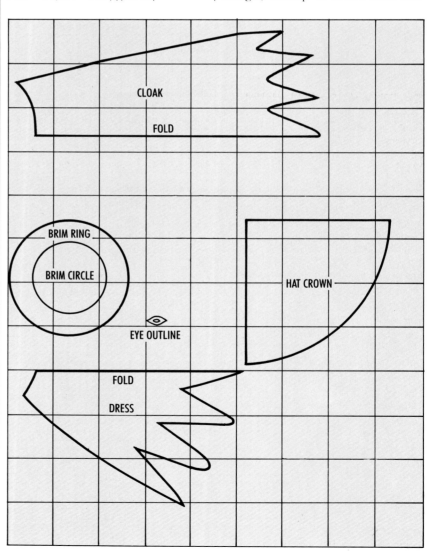

CLOAK

FOLD

BRIM RING

BRIM CIRCLE

EYE OUTLINE

HAT CROWN

FOLD

DRESS

catchstitch together. Slide pointed crown on to head. Pin and catchstitch to stocking fabric and wadding. Position stiffened brim over point of hat and settle at edge of hat. Pin and catchstitch.

8 To decorate face, using non-spirit base adhesive, glue two felt eye outlines and small stars in position for eyes. Press stalk of lime fruit into polystyrene head for nose. Sew on large round sequin centrally for mouth, securing it with the small bead.

9 Bend chenille serpent round neck to form a curly scarf look.

10 Catchstitch chenille frog to hat.

11 To make the broom, snip two thirds of the way into the width of the brown felt oblong. Roll round one end of covered black dowelling. Pin and catchstitch to hold. Catchstitch broom to front of dress as photograph.

CAKE FRILL

materials

32 cm (12½ in) of 115 cm (45 in)-wide black-and-white gingham
10 cm (4 in) of 82 cm (32¼ in)-wide craft-quality vilene
6 cm (2⅜ in) of 1.5 cm (⅝ in)-wide velcro
12 thin black pipecleaners 17 cm (6½ in) long
6 × 2 cm (¾ in)-diameter black acrylic pom-pons
1.5 m (1¾ yd) of 3 mm (⅛ in)-wide red double satin ribbon
matching thread (black)

to make

1 Cut the following:
from gingham 15 cm (6 in) by the circumference of your cake plus 5 cm (2 in) (for the fabric band), 8 cm (3 in) by twice the circumference of your cake (for the frill)
from vilene 6.5 cm (2½ in) by the circumference of your cake plus 5 cm (2 in) (for the band)

2 Mark notches by folding fabric band in half lengthways and marking centre at each end. On one end, mark a notch 5 cm (2 in) from the end on each long side. On other end, mark a notch 1 cm (⅜ in) from end on each long side.

3 Position one long edge of the vilene strip to wrong side of fabric band on centre notch mark. Pin, tack and

machine stitch 6 mm (¼ in) from centre edge.

4 Tear apart the velcro strip and position hook half vertically 1 cm (⅜ in) in on outside band of fabric, working through the two thicknesses. Pin, tack and machine stitch.

Position loop half on opposite end inside band, on fabric only. Pin, tack and machine stitch. Remove tacking.

5 Neaten short ends of frill with 6 mm (¼ in) turnings. Pin, tack and machine stitch. Fold frill piece in half lengthways. Set machine on the largest stitch length and run a double line of stitching 2 mm (¹⁄₁₆ in) and 6 mm (¼ in) from double raw edges. Pull up frill and fit between the 5 cm (2 in) and 1 cm (⅜ in) notches on fabric band, matching raw edges of frill to raw edge of band. Pin, tack and machine stitch with 1 cm (⅜ in) turnings. Remove tacking. Press 1 cm (⅜ in) turnings on the short ends of the fabric band to the wrong side; pin and catchstitch to hold in position.

6 Fold fabric 'lining' of band over to cover the vilene. Pin, tack and catchstitch short ends together. Turning 1 cm (⅜ in) to wrong side of remaining long edge, pin and catchstitch to base of frill. Lightly press the band only.

to decorate

1 Cut the twelve black pipecleaners in half. Form a star shape by criss-crossing four halves of pipecleaners. Holding the star shape in the centre, twist once to intertwine. Catchstitch centre to hold. Pin and catchstitch to a black pom-pon body.

2 Bend pipecleaner at halfway point to form 'knees' and bend approximately 1.5 cm (⅝ in) from ends to form 'feet'. Position spiders at 10 cm (4 in) intervals along cake frill. Catchstitch one foot on each of the spiders with black thread. Tie ribbon bows to each spider.

AFTERCARE

Gifts made with love need special care. Some of the items in this book require careful cleaning. Any which are not listed cannot be cleaned.

Rainbow theatre page 14
Clean with a damp cloth if necessary.
Storage: Lift the pole off the hooks above the door and roll theatre around pole. Remove the card stage and slip it inside the roll. The roll can then stand on one end inside a cupboard (or behind the door). It would be a good idea to wrap the roll in an old sheet.

Transport puppets page 20
Brush very gently with a lightly dampened sponge if necessary.

Cat and kitten bedcover page 23
Machine wash on a gentle cycle. Press carefully with a warm iron, avoiding the embroidered areas.

Bibs page 26
These are hand washable, but sponging them down gently after each use is really the best idea.

Ice cream mobile page 28
If the mobile gets dusty from hanging in a child's room, blow gently to remove loose dust and dip polyester wadding tops into warm water mixed with a small amount of washing-up liquid. Shake excess water off gently and rehang mobile.

PVC painting clothes page 32
Hand wash in warm soapy water, rinse and hang to drip dry. The gingham square can be machine washed.

Animal masks page 35
If stored in plastic bags, these should not need to be washed or cleaned.

Swimming pack page 39
Hand wash in mild soapy water. Pat into shape and dry on a flat surface.

Knitted hats page 43
Hand wash the hats in mild soapy water, then use a gentle fabric conditioner on them. Pat into shape and dry on a flat surface.

Dog pyjama case page 44
Dry clean to ensure that the variety of fabrics used do not bleed or shrink.

Messenger birds page 46
Blow dust away gently if necessary. To pack these birds as gifts (or to store them), place them in a flat box and pad them with crumpled tissue paper to support the stands.

Scottie dog cushion page 54
Remove Scottie dogs from cushion cover and machine wash on a gentle cycle. Press with a warm iron and re-attach Scotties.

Scottie dog slippers page 54
Hand wash in mild soapy water and dry flat.

Boy's travel roll page 56
Hand wash in mild soapy water. Pat into shape and dry the travel roll flat.

Rainbow slippers page 59
Hand wash in mild soapy water, then use a gentle fabric conditioner. Shape gently by hand and dry flat.

Ticking shoe bags page 62
Hand wash in mild soapy water. Pat flat to dry.

Fish bedcover page 65
Machine wash on a gentle cycle. Press carefully with a warm iron. Use a pressing cloth to iron the nylon net 'scales'.

Director's chair page 68
If necessary, the seat can be washed on a gentle cycle. Remove the wooden bars first!

Deckchair and bag page 70
The deckchair can be spot-cleaned if necessary. Hand wash the bag in mild soapy water and dry flat.

Celebration tablecloth page 74
Secure the scattered leaves to the cloth and gently hand wash in warm soapy liquid.
Do not wash the garland. If an individual leaf on the garland is stained, simply cut it away and replace. Check the garland for food and drink stains before

wrapping it well in acid-free tissue for safe storage.

Church posy page 76
Remove stains with a spot remover liquid. Store wrapped in tissue paper.

Christening set page 78
Dry cleaning is recommended for all pieces. Before cleaning, remove all detachable doves and finely oversew all those which are attached with bondaweb.
Storage: Air after dry cleaning. Fill the skirt with white tissue and place layers of tissue between the dress, bib, bonnet and shawl. Store in a sealed cardboard box. Never cover with polythene.

Butterfly cot cover page 83
Remove butterflies carefully and machine wash on a gentle cycle. Dry flat and catchstitch butterflies in place.

Cot toy with bells page 85
Unthread the ribbons and remove the bells. Gently hand wash the felt birds in warm soapy water. Reassemble when the birds are thoroughly dry.

Pearl sequin cushion page 94
Dry clean the cover if necessary.

Crystal serviette set page 95
Remove crystal beads carefully and hand wash gently, or machine wash on a gentle cycle in a pillowcase. When dry and well aired, attach the beads again.
Storage: Place the serviettes and rings between layers of white tissue paper.

Dog coat page 100
Hand wash in mild soapy water. Dry flat.

Dog towel page 101
Machine wash on a low temperature to keep colour from bleeding.

Cat mat page 102
Sponge clean after each feed. Hand wash in mild soapy water once a week or so.

Bird cage cover page 104
Dry clean if necessary. You may have to replace some of the acrylic pom-pons.

Advent tree and Snowman advent calendar pages 108 and 110
Barring unforeseen accidents, these decorations should not need to be cleaned more often than every few years. Remove sequins, fruits, etc., and dry clean when necessary.
Storage: If possible, hang them on coat hangers and pin sheets of white tissue to cover them completely. Store hanging in a wardrobe cupboard. Never cover with polythene as moisture will collect and cause mildew to form if there is a temperature change.

Christmas door decoration and Thanksgiving garland pages 112 and 128
With correct use, these should not need to be cleaned. Storage: Line a suitable sized cardboard box with white tissue paper and cover the ring with more tissue. Seal the lid of the box with tape.

Appliqué tablecloth page 113
Hand wash in warm soapy water or machine wash on a gentle cycle. Place the tablecloth and serviettes in a pillow case for protection if washing in the machine. Press with a warm iron.
Storage: Store serviettes flat and the tablecloth folded and lined with tissue paper in a cardboard box.

Christmas apron page 114
Remove strips of seed heads and sponge the apron clean. To store, roll seed head strip in white tissue paper and fold the apron between layers of tissue.

Christmas table set page 116
Remove strips of seed heads and gently hand wash the mats, coasters and rings in warm soapy water.

Easter table set page 122
Sponge mats and serviette rings clean after each use. Hand wash occasionally if necessary and dry flat. Machine wash the serviettes and press with a hot iron.

Duck cosies page 124
Remove duck, bow tie and lining from tea cosy. Gently hand wash each piece separately in warm soapy water. Dry flat. The lining could be machine washed on a gentle cycle if necessary. Lightly hand wash the egg cosies in the same way and dry flat.

Halloween slippers, mobile and witch puppets pages 130, 133, 134
These may all finish the day somewhat the worse for wear. If not, store them wrapped in tissue paper in a cardboard box.

Cake frill page 135
Remove the spiders carefully and hand wash the gingham band in warm soapy water. Dry flat, press with a medium iron and sew the spiders on again. Store flat wrapped in white tissue paper.

GLOSSARY

Appliqué
A decorative sewing technique in which fabrics of different shapes are applied, or placed, on a background fabric to create a totally new design. The edges are held in position with tiny stitches that should be hardly seen, or by a decorative embroidery stitch such as buttonhole stitch or a machined zig-zag stitch.

Bag out
A sewing technique in which two shaped pieces are stitched with right sides together and turned right sides out to create a firm, neatly finished edge. The double-sided fabric shapes can then be applied to a background fabric.

Bias binding
Strips of bias-cut fabric lengths used to bind off the edges of many sewn items. It is a useful technique for finishing soft furnishings and clothing. It can be bought in a wide range of colours in several widths in cotton or polyester, or self-binding can be made to match any item.

Bondaweb
A soft iron-on adhesive web used to bond fabrics together securely. It has a special paper backing which makes it easy to handle and cut. It is especially useful for appliqué work and for making double-sided shapes that do not fray. It is also handy for repairing tears, rips, etc.

Broderie anglaise
A kind of embroidery which is used to trim the edge of lace, hems, etc, which is characterised by a scalloped edge and a series of tiny openings which are bound with buttonhole stitch.

Casing
A tubular opening such as a waistband through which a drawstring or length of elastic can be threaded to make a garment fit or to close the top of a bag or purse.

Catchstitch
A technique which involves taking tiny stitches by hand, usually on the right side of the item being sewn, to hold a motif or other applied piece of decorative

fabric in place almost invisibly.

Fabric grain
See Grain.

Fingerpress
To rub hard with the fingers along a seam or edge of an item being sewn to press it temporarily in order to continue working.

Fuse
To join two or more pieces of fabric together, usually by ironing them to a piece of fusible webbing. (See Bondaweb.)

Grain
The line of the warp, or lengthways, thread on a piece of fabric.

Gathering
The technique of pulling together a length of fabric into folds or wrinkles by stitching through it with a long running thread and puckering the fabric into frills or ruffles.

Hem
The finished border of a piece of fabric made by turning the edge under and stitching it down, either by hand or by machine.

Mitre
A method of joining two straight edges to a piece of fabric at a right angle, made by joining the corners at angles of 45°. The technique is especially useful for finishing the edges of tablecloths, mats, serviettes, etc.

Motif
A decorative feature which is applied separately to garments or soft furnishings.

Notch(es)
V-shaped marks made on the edges of various pieces of items to be sewn. They provide a way of matching the pieces in the right order and at the right place.

Oversew
To stitch securely along the edge of a seam or an applied motif. Oversewing can be done with a zig-zag

machine stitch, but is more usually done neatly by hand.

Piping
A decorative method of edging, carried out by enclosing a length of cord in a continuous length of matching or contrasting fabric and applying it to the border of garments, soft furnishings or motifs.

Rouleau
A hollow tube of fabric usually used for covering wires etc., for making frog-type buttonholes or for decoration.

Sandwich
To combine layers of fabric, wadding, vilene, etc, and stitch them together by hand or machine.

Selvedge
The woven lengthwise edges of a bolt of fabric constructed so that the material does not fray. In most cases, it should be removed before the cloth is used.

Snip
To cut tiny nicks into the edge of curved seams without cutting through the seamline stitching, in order to provide 'ease' or 'give' to the seam.

Straight grain
See Grain.

Tack(ing)
To stitch together two or more pieces of fabric loosely to hold them in position while more permanent stitching is carried out. The tacking stitches are usually removed after the final stitching has been done.

Teflon foot
A sewing machine attachment designed to allow the needle to slide smoothly and freely over slick surfaces such as PVC.

Topstitch
To stitch along the extreme edge of a finished border or edge of an assembled item or motif. It acts as both a decorative finish and a secure way of attaching one piece of fabric to another. Top stitching is usually done by machine on a fairly tight straight stitch.

Tubular
Tube-like; a long narrow piece of fabric which is open at one or both ends. (See Casing.)

Turnings
The seam allowance on the edges of fabric pieces to be joined. Standard turnings range from 1 cm (⅜ in) to 1.5 cm (¾ in).

Velcro
Touch-and-close fastening made of two strips of nylon.

One strip consists of tiny loops, the other of tiny barbed hooks. It provides an easy-to-open method of attaching two pieces of fabric together.

Vilene
A non-woven fabric backing or interlining used to provide body on garments, toys and soft furnishings.

Wadding
A thick, non-woven polyester padding substance used to provide warmth to outer garments, quilts, etc, and to give depth to padded items. It can also be used to stuff small decorative items, toys, etc.

Warp
The threads in woven cloth that run lengthways on the loom. The warp threads are strung on the loom and the crossways threads are woven through them.

Weft
The crossways threads in a woven cloth. They are woven under and over the lengthways, or warp, threads.

Zig-zag
A strong decorative stitch which makes a chevron pattern. It is especially useful for applying motifs to background fabrics securely and attractively and to finishing the edges of seams, etc, to prevent fraying.

Zipper foot
A sewing machine attachment designed to keep the needle running smoothly along a zip. It keeps the teeth of the zip clear of the needle and is also useful for attaching piping cord, etc.

ACKNOWLEDGEMENTS

The author would like to thank the following suppliers:
Chartwell True-Sew, HW Peel & Co. Ltd, Greenford Middx (centimetre pattern paper); Elna (GB) Ltd, Queens House, 180-2 Tottenham Court Rd, London W1 (sewing machine); Laura Ashley Ltd, 27 Bagley's Lane, London SW6 (bias bindings); Lorettas Crafts, 15 Sundown Ave, Dunstable, Beds (handicraft equipment); John Lewis plc, Oxford St, London W1 (fabric and PVC); Perivale-Gutermann Ltd, Wadsworth Rd, Greenford, Middx (threads); Selectus Ltd, Biddulph, Stoke-on-Trent, Staffs (velcro); The Vilene Organisation, Greetland, Halifax, W. Yorks (interfacings); B Brown (Holbourn) Ltd, Warriner House, 32-3 Greville St, London EC1 (felts and laminates).

The publishers would like to thank the following shops for their kindness in providing items used in the photography in this book:
Complete Cookshop, Windsor, Berks (cutlery and cookware); Country Furniture, Windsor, Berks (furniture); Country Style Flowers, Windsor, Berks (Easter basket); Ewers, Windsor, Berks (dog lead, dog basket, cat bowl); O'Connor Bros., Windsor, Berks (furniture); The Picture Frame Workshop, Windsor, Berks (prints); The Pine Place, Windsor, Berks (furniture); The Token House, Windsor, Berks (crockery, glassware); Turk's Head Antiques, Eton, Berks (silver dish); Windsor Bedding Centre, Windsor, Berks (bedhead); Woodward and Stalder Ltd, Windsor, Berks (sports goods).

INDEX

141